THE PERFORMANCE MANAGEMENT REVOLUTION

THE PERFORMANCE MANAGEMENT REVOLUTION

Business Results Through Insight and Action

HOWARD DRESNER

1807
WILEY
2007

JOHN WILEY & SONS, INC.

Library of Congress Cataloging-in-Publication Data:

Dresner, Howard, 1957-
   The performance management revolution: business results through insight and action/ Howard Dresner.
      p. cm.
   Includes index.
   ISBN 978-0-470-12483-3 (cloth)
   1.   Management information systems.   2.   Information technology—Management.
3.   Performance—Management.   I. Title.
   HD30.213.D74 2008
   658.4'038011—dc22   2007023152

To my wife, Patty
And to my children—Sarah, Joshua, and Ethan

Contents

Foreword

Some revolutions—like the American Revolution—are bloody, noisy, and everyone nearby knows about them. Others—like the Industrial Revolution—are quieter, slower, and many people at the time may not even realize they're happening. In the long run, though, both kinds of revolutions lead to profound change.

Today, I believe we are in the early stages of one of the quiet revolutions. At the heart of this revolution is an increase in human freedom in business.

Key enablers for this revolution are the increasing availability of information and new technology that helps people act on it. When people have access to more information, they can make more sensible decisions. They don't have to wait for orders from someone above them in a hierarchy who supposedly knows more than they do. And when they have the freedom to make decisions and the ability to take action for themselves, they are often more highly motivated, more creative, and more flexible.

In our increasingly knowledge-based and innovation-driven economy, these benefits of decentralized decision making—motivation, creativity, and flexibility—are often the critical factors in business success. And that's why I believe this increase in human freedom in business will spread throughout many parts of our economy. In the long run,

I think it will be as important a change for business as the change to democracies was for governments.

But what does this really mean for you?

Of all the businesspeople I know, Howard Dresner has some of the deepest insights into the practical implications of this revolution. In the eloquently written book you're about to read, you'll see how Dresner's concept of Information Democracy has profound implications for the way your company can operate. You'll see how a new generation of performance management software enables Information Democracy. And you'll see how all this leads to a new way of managing companies in the first place: empowered individuals at all levels working collaboratively toward shared objectives, with full knowledge of how their own actions affect performance.

Will everything be different after this revolution? No, of course not. When a country changes from a kingdom to a democracy, many aspects of daily life don't change at all. But there are profound changes in some aspects of political life: where power comes from, how it is exercised, and what the country's leaders try to do.

In the same way, many aspects of daily life in business won't change in the business revolution we're now entering. But there will be profound changes in how we use information, how decisions are made, and in some of our basic assumptions about management.

This book provides a compelling and insightful description of what these changes will really mean for you and how you can take advantage of them to improve your business performance.

Thomas W. Malone
Patrick J. McGovern Professor of Management
Director, Center for Collective Intelligence
Sloan School of Management
Massachusetts Institute of Technology

Preface

This book is about the coming revolution in performance management in global enterprises.

Throughout human history, revolutions have led to radical changes in the governments, economic systems, social structures, and even the cultural values of nation states. The American Revolution of the late 1700s, for example, achieved the political separation of the 13 colonies in North America from the British Empire and led to a new form of democracy with respect for individual rights and property at its center.

The ancient Greeks took a rather dim view of revolution, believing it to be the result of an undesirable breakdown in social values and structures. It wasn't until the Renaissance that revolution acquired a more positive image, coming to be viewed as a sometimes necessary means of achieving freedom or advancing a cause.

Regardless of whether their outcomes are positive or negative, successful revolutions always result in fundamental and often irreversible changes in the established order. The coming revolution in performance management will be no different, resulting in fundamental and very likely irreversible changes in how organizations approach organizing and providing access to information, planning and implementing performance management initiatives, and using technology to support these activities.

Perhaps the most dramatic outcome of the performance management revolution will be the ascendancy of a new management system for the global enterprise in the 21st century. This modern management system will consist of people, processes, and technologies unified and optimized to achieve higher levels of performance and accountability. It will empower individuals to make decisions and take action on their own; define management processes to support increasingly decentralized organizational structures; and include technology that supports people and processes day to day while providing a platform for long-term business growth.

Central to this modern management system is a way of organizing and providing access to information I call Information Democracy. Information Democracy is a principle of equality that demands actionable insight for all. When it is achieved, everyone in even the largest organizations has all the information they need to make decisions without having to rely on someone from Information Technology (IT) to give it to them and without being filtered or censored by management. At the heart of Information Democracy is the ability of everyone to access data, turn it into knowledge and insight through analysis, and share that insight with others.

Anyone who has ever worked in a large organization will recognize what I've just described as a radical departure from how information is used—and sometimes abused—in organizations today. Too often, information is locked away in complex systems accessible only to experts and reserved for an elite few, making it hard for the people who are primarily responsible for managing performance in a business day to day to get their jobs done.

Revolutions are typically sparked by prolonged and deep dissatisfaction with the status quo. As I travel the world talking with executives and managers in organizations about performance management, this is often what I hear about the state of information in organizations today:

"I'm sick and tired of not having the right information to do my job and having to guess at what it is."

"I'm sick and tired of multiple, inconsistent answers to a single question."

"I'm sick and tired of people hoarding information."

"I'm sick and tired of our inability to act quickly and decisively when business conditions change."

"I'm sick and tired of complex systems and tools that are virtually impossible to use."

"I'm sick and tired of spending more time in meetings arguing over the data than deciding what to do about it."

These and similar complaints amount to nothing less than an indictment of the way organizations treat information. And as a student of history—and a long-time technology revolutionary—I am convinced that we are on the brink of a long-overdue revolution.

As for the desired outcome of this revolution, I would put it this way: We seek common business truth and understanding across the entire organization and for all users with the objective of aligning everyone with the mission of the enterprise in a meaningful way.

I've addressed the questions of "why" and "what," but there remains the question of "why now?" What is it about the current business climate that has created a sense of urgency about solving problems that have existed for decades?

Here is what I believe. Just a few years into the 21st century, the world already seems a very different place. U.S. and global populations are growing—and growing increasingly diverse, dynamic, and interdependent. Technology and the Internet are permanently blurring—and often dissolving—geographic, economic, and cultural borders. And global geopolitical tensions are raising the stakes for all nations to live together peacefully and productively.

While these extraordinary factors have profound implications for our daily lives, their impact on business is equally profound. Globalization and the hypercompetition it fosters, technology with all its promises and challenges, and geopolitical uncertainties that keep us in a permanent state of anxiety about external forces over which we have no control combine to create a harsh and unforgiving business climate. And thanks to the ethical lapses of a few high-profile corporations and executives in the early 2000s, regulatory scrutiny of financial and accounting practices is at an all-time high.

In this new century, many organizations struggle to meet—let alone anticipate—their stakeholders' objectives. At the same time, they are under increasing pressure to maintain strong corporate controls and offer greater degrees of transparency. Misaligned strategies, outdated plans, and unreliable forecasts inhibit success. Many businesses depend on performance measures that lack consistency and do not reflect structural business drivers. Most cannot reliably understand the past in time to make decisions about the future.

As a result, executives and managers are being asked to assimilate vast amounts of information and adopt new management techniques such as Economic Value Added (EVA), Balanced Scorecard, virtual close, event-driven planning, Six Sigma, and rolling forecasts, to name just a few. They are being asked to incorporate evolving legal reporting and disclosure regulations, constantly revise plans, participate in extended business models that include partners in other organizations, and leverage investments in existing business systems.

The situation is further compounded by the presence of multiple, stand-alone systems in most organizations—often distributed across different countries of operation—that fail to present a unified picture of the business, support collaboration between teams, or drive the execution of frequently revised plans.

How can organizations reconcile the enormous pressures they face with the increasingly difficult task of generating the growth in stakeholder value that these same market conditions offer? A large part of the answer lies in adopting the right tools for the job. And among the right tools is Enterprise Performance Management (EPM).

EPM is a relatively new category of enterprise software that replaces the tools organizations use today to manage performance—often spreadsheets and static reports—with more flexible, scalable, and dynamic tools. EPM goes beyond the specific functions automated by transactional systems—accounting, billings, bookings, supply chain, sales force automation, and call centers. Consisting of a consolidation, planning and analytics platform, and financial and business applications, EPM uses data from the transactional systems to increase visibility, drive forecasts, predict results, manage financial and operational performance, and report on outcomes both internally and externally.

Especially as part of a modern management system for the global enterprise—adding the technology piece to the people, processes, and technology triad—EPM gives executives, managers, and knowledge workers deep insight into their businesses today and tools for improving performance tomorrow. With EPM, companies can actively manage their success.

And, while the desire for better solutions to actively manage performance is the primary driver of EPM, it turns out that EPM has other benefits as well.

For example, better access to better quality information—a hallmark of EPM—enables organizations to move away from using purely financial metrics for gauging performance to a broader range of value-based and balanced indicator approaches. These broader measurements are especially effective at linking strategic objectives to operational drivers and managing the discrepancy between the market and book value of businesses. Many organizations are having success using these techniques, especially as they mature and build a critical mass of experiences and well-trained talent.

EPM also adds value to organizations' existing transactional systems by unlocking information trapped in them and making it available to decision makers. Transactional systems increase efficiency by streamlining operational processes and generating large quantities of valuable data, but many organizations find themselves with multiple systems due to acquisitions, mergers, or the autonomous nature of their business units or geographies. Often, these systems are not integrated with one another, which makes it difficult to gain access and share valuable data.

Support for increasingly decentralized organizational structures is another added value of EPM. More organizations today are adopting strategies that involve using shared services, outsourcing, or a network of business partners to extend their capabilities. These strategies require more flexible ways of organizing and managing processes that can adapt to an open and fluid organizational model.

As it becomes clear that EPM can address these and many other issues challenging organizations, interest in the category has expanded. But organizations can be slow to change. That is why a revolution in performance management is brewing, and why, in my view, it is necessary. It is brewing in finance departments, business units, and executive suites. It is brewing in businesses in all industries. It is brewing in geographies all over the world. And it can't be stopped.

Still, revolution is hard work. I know this from experience. I spent 13 years at Gartner, the world's largest IT advisory company, and have been Chief Strategy Officer at Hyperion. As a research fellow and a lead analyst for Business Intelligence (BI) while at Gartner and even before then, I had a chance to be part of—and even instigate— some exciting technology revolutions of my own.

In 1989, for example, I started—some might say incited—the BI revolution with the premise that all users have a fundamental right to access information without the help of IT. Just a few years later, in 1993, I expanded that premise into the concept of Information Democracy. Since then, the industry has made modest progress toward achieving Information Democracy, but we're not there yet, and frankly, we have a long way to go.

And so in this book, I offer executives and managers insight into what my fellow revolutionaries and I have learned in our push for Information Democracy and other essential components of more effective performance management. My hope is that if you haven't already joined the performance management revolution, you will after reading this book.

Remember, though, revolution is not the endgame. Information Democracy isn't even the endgame. Both are means to an end—the realization of a new management system for global enterprises in the 21st century—one that empowers individuals and puts organizations on a path to better performance through insight and action.

Let the revolution begin.

Howard Dresner
May 2007

Acknowledgments

I am grateful to many colleagues and friends who contributed ideas, information, and facts to this book.

I especially want to acknowledge my colleagues at Hyperion, whose knowledge and expertise were invaluable in writing this book. Ron Dimon deserves special thanks for his tireless work in getting this project off the ground and his many contributions along the way. I would also like to thank John Kopcke, Rick Cadman, John O'Rourke, Frank Buytendijk, and Phyllis Davidson for their ideas and contributions; Kathy Horton, Toby Hatch, and the other Domain Leads for their contribution to the chapter that includes an EPM self-assessment; and Godfrey Sullivan for his leadership.

My gratitude goes to Dr. Raef Lawson for his research and content on creating Centers of Excellence.

I benefited from the project management, writing, and editing skills of Susan Thomas. Her participation made writing this book easier and more fun than I could have imagined.

I owe a debt to Tom Malone, certainly for the foreword to this book, but also for his keen insights and groundbreaking work in demonstrating how technology can make our work and personal lives richer and more productive.

I want to thank my agent, Susan Barry, for her instincts about how to package my ideas and whose efforts quickly led to a publishing contract. My editor, Tim Burgard, offered valuable feedback and encouragement along the way.

All the companies mentioned in this book have helped bring its concepts to life. Named and unnamed, their participation was critical. I especially want to thank Daniel M. Morales of Bank of America, Spencer Taft and Neil Johnston of Cox Enterprises, and Michael Benjamin of Pearson.

To my wife Patty, my daughter Sarah, and my sons Joshua and Ethan: thank you for your love and unwavering support. They mean everything to me.

THE PERFORMANCE MANAGEMENT REVOLUTION

Part One

A CALL TO ARMS

∼ 1 ∼

The Need for Change

In his 2004 book, *The Future of Work,* Thomas W. Malone, the Patrick J. McGovern professor of management at the MIT Sloan School of Management and the author of the foreword to this book, wrote about a dramatic shift that is occurring in how businesses are organized. According to Malone, the first and second stages of the shift are already mostly complete, as large, centralized corporate hierarchies have come to replace small, informally organized businesses over the last 200 years.

There is a third stage, however—one in which corporate hierarchies evolve to more decentralized business networks—and it's just beginning. In this stage, enabled by technologies that drive down the cost of communications, large corporations actually shrink in size through a combination of outsourcing and vertical disintegration. Through outsourcing and vertical disintegration, big companies off-load work to contractors and create networks of separate but interrelated businesses. These business networks perform much of the work that previously has been done inside large organizations.

Malone often cites eBay as a prime example of a company that operates as a business network. Today, several hundred thousand eBay sellers around the world make their full-time living on eBay. If these people were employees of eBay, the company would be one of the largest global employers and retailers in the world. But eBay sellers are independent business people.

This way of organizing delivers huge benefits to eBay, which can grow bigger and faster with fewer resources than traditionally organized companies. But it also creates new and interesting challenges. Because eBay has less control over its direct business activity than many other companies, it must take into account opinions from both sellers and buyers in the eBay network before making many of its decisions.

This increase in what Malone calls human freedom in business—where employees, suppliers, partners, contractors, and even customers get to have a say in how organizations are run—is just one of the many changes that result as businesses decentralize.

But even before the emergence of radical new business structures such as the one exemplified by eBay, the trend toward decentralization in business gave rise to changes in the roles employees play in organizations—especially employees whose main contributions depend on the productive use of information instead of manual labor.

Nearly 50 years ago, Peter Drucker coined the term "knowledge worker" to describe this category of employee. Back then, Drucker predicted that knowledge workers would grow as a proportion of the total workforce, becoming its "center of gravity" and forever changing the nature of organizations, management, and work.

Drucker was right. Today, knowledge workers are an increasingly large percentage of the global workforce, especially in developed countries. Across all industries, knowledge workers represent at least 25 percent of the workforce, and in financial services, health care, high tech, and media, the percentage is even higher.

And today, knowledge workers perform many of the key frontline activities in organizations. In so doing, they have become primarily responsible for driving day-to-day performance in business—fulfilling another Drucker prophecy. In his 1966 book, *The Effective Executive,* Drucker wrote, "Every knowledge worker in modern organization is an 'executive' if, by virtue of his position or knowledge, he is responsible for a contribution that materially affects the capacity of the organization to perform and to obtain results."

WHAT'S WRONG WITH THIS PICTURE?

You would think that with more than 50 years to think about it—a time span in which knowledge workers evolved into the key managers of day-to-day performance in organizations and technology has enabled access to information and better, faster, cheaper communication—organizations would have figured out how to provide their people with the information and tools they need to do their jobs.

Yet, in most organizations today, people waste countless hours searching for the data they need—even when it resides in their own companies. Countless more hours are wasted trying to coordinate their work with others. The fact that the volume of corporate email—the communication tool of choice in business—has risen to 35 billion a day from just 10 billion a day five years ago is testimony to the difficulty of this task. And just imagine how many of those emails include spreadsheet attachments.

There is something wrong with a picture of modern business that shows people in critical positions struggling to get the information they need to do their jobs. But there is an explanation for it. Many organizations today are still coming to terms with the changes in their businesses so eloquently described by experts such as Thomas Malone, Peter Drucker, and others. And they are still using models of management designed for large, centralized organizations and using management systems—people, processes, and technology—that support these outdated models.

Organizations' technology investments reflect this disconnect between modern organizational structures and outdated management models. Here is one example.

Over the past two decades, companies have poured hundreds of millions of dollars into transactional systems, especially enterprise resource management (ERP) systems. As a result, most businesses today can take orders, fill orders, generate invoices, populate a general ledger, and so on with great efficiency—all of which are critical to running a large business.

But *managing* a large business is an entirely different endeavor. While it may start with the same data at the same level of granularity as running a business, managing a business requires access to value-added information—raw data that has been transformed, analyzed, and presented to individuals who use a variety of management processes appropriate to their organizations to make decisions and take actions from a variety of perspectives. Managing a business is, by definition, a dynamic activity requiring flexible processes and tools that are different for every organization and that can adapt to change over time.

But because the purpose of ERP systems is to perform and store vast amounts of mission-critical transactions, they are inflexible—by design. And ERP systems automate processes that are inflexible—by design. In fact, once these systems are in place and working well, organizations will do just about anything—including changing the way people work—*not* to have to change them. And while they generate large amounts of valuable data, most organizations have many ERP systems—a dozen or more—that are not integrated.

To cite just one example: A multibillion dollar European provider of retail and wholesale services with 120 business units across seven divisions and operations in seven countries has more than 20 ERP or accounting systems. In companies such as this—typical of businesses its size and scope—reconciling so many different views of reality is a challenge—a challenge, by the way, the company has mastered.

Viewed this way, it's clear that what's needed for organizations to manage performance is the mirror opposite of what transactional systems deliver: flexibility. They need flexible processes and technologies because managing performance today is a dynamic activity full of complexity and nuance.

Bottom line, ERP systems help organizations *run* their business by standardizing and automating high-volume, transactional business processes across an organization. But they do little or nothing to help them *manage* their business.

A SIMPLE MODEL FOR A SIMPLE BUSINESS

To gain greater insight into what is needed to manage a business, let's consider the example of a single-proprietor candy store.

In a single-proprietor candy store, the owner likely does everything associated with managing the business, including front room and back office functions. For example, he observes firsthand the makeup of his customer base and their buying patterns. He knows which customers prefer which products and how often they buy them. He knows when he is serving a repeat customer or a new one. He knows which of his products are more popular with his customers than others are. And he knows when customers are asking for products he doesn't carry.

Because it's a business managed by one person, information can be quickly analyzed and incorporated back into strategy and decision making. He may decide that he needs to increase his inventory of some products and decrease others. He may decide to start carrying new products for which there is demand. And after having made decisions like these, he can evaluate whether they were good or bad ones and make midcourse corrections, if necessary, in a very short period of time. The activities and processes required to run his business are simple and straightforward and, since the owner is the only person who uses them, they don't need to be documented.

But what happens if the owner hires a counter clerk or a bookkeeper so he can spend less time in the store? Or decides to open another candy store in the next town?

As soon as more than one person works in his business, the owner must formally define, possibly modify, and definitely document critical management activities and processes. He must do this because he can no longer personally observe and take part in everything that goes on in his business. He must do this because he wants to make sure his business is managed in the right way even when he is not around. For all its elegance and simplicity, the single-proprietor candy store model just doesn't scale.

However, there are lessons to be learned here that apply to all businesses of all sizes. And regardless of scale, we must all strive to attain the customer intimacy and business agility of the single-proprietor candy store.

∽ 2 ∽

A Model for a Modern Management System

In theory, there is no difference in the activities required to manage a single-proprietor candy store and those required to manage a business of 100, 1,000, or even 100,000 employees. Regardless of the size of the business, managing it requires four basic activities coming together in what I call the management cycle: vision and strategy; goal and objective setting; execution; and evaluation (see Exhibit 2.1).

Ideally, the activities in this management cycle should support the purpose of the organization, the means of achieving it, and its ability to adapt. But in actual practice—and especially as businesses grow in size—these activities can quickly become unsynchronized and end up in conflict with one another. For example, in many large organizations, functional departments, and geographic regions disregard corporate strategy in favor of local and parochial considerations. And oftentimes, strategy becomes disconnected from reality, as those who create the strategy are removed from the customers and markets they supposedly serve.

EXHIBIT 2.1 The Management Cycle

CONNECTING THE CYCLE

Ideally, these activities would not exist in isolation from each other and would not occur sequentially. Instead, they would have well-defined processes to connect them and support the flow of work between them. And they would unfold iteratively, creating cycles within the cycle. The "connective" processes necessary to make this possible are rationalization, commitment, tracking, and perspective (see Exhibit 2.2).

Rationalization

Once vision and strategy have been established, an organization should go through a process of rationalization to ensure that the strategy is attainable and realistic before setting goals. Managers might ask, "Does the organization have ample resources (capital, expertise, and so on) to achieve the strategy? Is the market nascent, supply driven, or demand driven? Can the organization develop the market or overcome current perceptions to compete successfully?" There will be a healthy amount of debate and negotiation in this enterprisewide conversation. Once a rationalization process

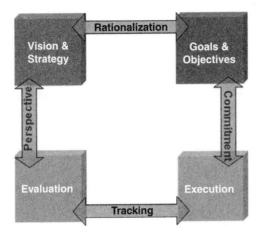

EXHIBIT 2.2 The Management Cycle and Connective Processes

is complete, an organization can set goals and objectives with confidence, knowing that they are achievable and support the organization's vision and strategy.

Commitment

Before an organization executes a strategy, it should collectively commit to specific areas of focus and deliverables. The commitment process documents the investments an organization will make (capital, people, materials, programs, and so on) and the expected outcomes, including revenue, expenses, profit, and market share. Once the commitment process is complete, an organization can begin executing.

Tracking

Tracking is a process that should be used during execution to provide an operational feedback loop. Tracking progress against stated goals and objectives enables an organization to constantly fine tune to ensure optimal performance.

Perspective

Perspective is a process an organization should adopt during the evaluation activity to ensure it has the most complete view possible of what worked and what didn't, and what must be changed in the future to improve performance. To borrow a phrase from Italian filmmaker Sergio Leone, perspective provides insight into "the good, the bad, and the ugly." Managers might ask, "What synergies in our business helped us achieve success? Were there areas of misalignment that caused problems? Are there best practices that worked in one area of our business that we should replicate across the entire organization?" An organization can use conclusions drawn during this phase to modify strategy to better map to market, customer, and organizational realities.

The four management cycle activities—vision and strategy, goal and objective setting, execution, and evaluation—combined with these connective processes form the basis of a modern management system.

PROBLEMS WITH THE STATUS QUO

All organizations have a management system; it would be impossible to function without one. However, many organizations' management systems are deeply flawed, and the problem often is that the connective processes between management activities are weak, inconsistent, unsynchronized, or in some cases, completely absent.

The problem usually begins with vision and strategy. In many organizations, senior management defines a strategy to support its vision based on past experience or gut feeling—or even just a strong desire to do things a certain way—without rationalizing or fully vetting it. When the rationalization process is flawed or nonexistent, every other activity in the management cycle is doomed to failure as the impact of a poorly thought-out strategy ripples throughout the organization.

For example, if the strategy is flawed, goals and objectives may not be attainable. If goals and objectives aren't attainable, those attempting to achieve them either abandon them for fear of failure or execute against a different strategy they believe will yield better results.

Another area where disconnects are common is between strategy, execution, and tracking. The strategy may be sound and execution crisp, but if the organization does not have access to meaningful information in the tracking process, it may be impossible to determine whether actions are resulting in the desired outcomes and if not, what must be done to correct the problems. Even the best information without context is useless.

This kind of disconnect is common in companies that rely on Business Intelligence (BI) alone to manage performance. BI is knowledge gained through the access and analysis of business information. BI tools and technologies include query and reporting, OLAP (online analytical processing), data mining and advanced analytics, end-user tools for ad hoc query and analysis, enterprise-class query, analysis and reporting, including dashboards for performance monitoring, and production reporting against enterprise data sources.

BI is of great value in managing performance, but has limitations in that its main purpose is to provide information about what happened and not much else. And too often, that information lacks context.

As an analogy, think of a soccer game and the role of a scoreboard. A scoreboard simply keeps track of the score. It doesn't tell spectators anything about the play action that led to the teams achieving that score. It doesn't provide any information to the coach of the trailing team that would help it catch up and overtake its opponent. It doesn't tell individual players what they can do to play better for the remainder of the game.

BI is the scoreboard of the enterprise and nothing more. It doesn't facilitate the business or improve it in any way. It does not provide context. It simply tells the score.

Not only is this partially useful, without the proper context it might be telling the score of something that has nothing at all to do with the ability of a business to achieve its goals. And even so, organizations need more than the score of the game to figure out what to do next.

For example, they need to know what they can do to improve their business. This requires more than reporting and analysis; it also takes management, and management requires planning, which is beyond the scope of BI.

Organizations also need to establish repeatability by moving from focusing on analytic processes to focusing on business processes. This requires an understanding of all the complexities of the business, which is also beyond the scope of BI.

Organizations also must foster accountability, which can only be achieved if they and the individuals who work in them know how to measure performance. Accountability requires documenting assumptions about the business, understanding what drives it, and making investments accordingly—another capability beyond the scope of BI.

TOWARD BETTER PROCESSES: EPM AND AN EPM SYSTEM

What's needed beyond transactional systems and BI are more capable tools and technologies that are part of and support a modern management system for the global enterprise in the 21st century. The tools and technologies must empower individuals in organizations through Information

Democracy, enable processes that support increasingly decentralized organizational structures, and provide a platform for growth.

This is where Enterprise Performance Management (EPM) technology comes in. EPM technology is enterprise software with applications and tools that drive management activities and processes forward with the agility to support their inherently dynamic nature.

EPM does this by fortifying the management cycle through support of the connective processes—rationalization, commitment, tracking, and perspective—with enterprise-class modeling, planning, BI, and analytics—fully integrated into a single system (see Exhibit 2.3).

Having these capabilities integrated into an EPM system is important, even though a number of EPM solutions today are packaged as integrated suites. The distinction is an all-important detail. Here's why.

A suite is a collection of programs—typically applications and some programming software of related functionality—that share a more or less common user

Exhibit 2.3 Activities and Connective Processes Supported by an EPM System

interface and have some capability to share data. The applications in most suites start out as stand-alone products and are often integrated and placed under a common user interface at a later date.

In contrast, a system is a group of interacting, interrelated, and interdependent elements that together form a unified whole.

As an analogy, consider music before iPod. Music lovers likely had a number of incompatible devices for listening to music, each of which had its own interface. The music they purchased came in different formats, and even if it was downloadable, was probably obtained from a variety of sites.

With iPod, music lovers can obtain everything they need to listen to whatever audio programming—and more recently, also movies and television programming—they desire by purchasing iPod and some accessories, and by downloading from the iTunes store. In the iPod "system," iTunes can become the single source for programming and iPod the single device for accessing programming. With a computer, music lovers can even create their own programming, store it on iTunes, and access it using their iPod. One environment . . . one interface . . . fully integrated for ease of use and deployment.

Organizations gain similar advantages when EPM is integrated into a system. They gain actionable insight and the ability to link strategies to plans, continuously monitor execution against goals, and drive higher levels of performance. They can share goals and progress with individuals responsible for achieving them. And individuals can share insight and information with management and their peers to ensure alignment. All through one environment . . . one interface . . . fully integrated for ease of use and deployment.

An EPM system is a logical next step for organizations seeking more advanced and effective performance management tools. This is because applications and tools that help people perform management activities and support management processes are good, but they are not good enough. All of these processes generate data that must be shared, and all of these processes are iterative and so they must be linked. Therefore, EPM must be integrated into a unified system that includes a user environment through which people access applications, tools, and the information they generate, and common services to ensure a common repository, integration and data sharing, and user provisioning.

In addition to tools for business users, the system must include tools for IT people who deploy and manage it.

To sum up, the role of an EPM system in a modern management system is to help *automate* the managerial activities and processes, to function as the connective fabric, and to make the complete cycle more effective, consistent, and reliable in supporting business performance.

THE MANAGEMENT SYSTEM AT GREENCO

For a model view of a modern management system supported by an EPM system, let's look at how the activities and processes that define the system play out at a hypothetical company: GreenCo.

Vision and Strategy

In the vision and strategy stage, top management literally determines the purpose of the enterprise and the high-level strategies the organization will adopt to realize its vision. In our example, the top management of GreenCo wants to change the way people live in the 21st century by helping them be more environmentally responsible.

To realize this vision, GreenCo intends to build a line of "green" products for homeowners such as alternative electricity generation devices, including photovoltaic panels and wind-driven power generators.

Rationalization with Modeling

Before GreenCo can reasonably set goals and objectives for this line of products, it must create models to test whether it is even feasible to do so.

Models are the rules of business, and if GreenCo is going to build and sell something, it needs rules for funding, designing, manufacturing, marketing, selling, delivering, and supporting it and so on. Models will tell GreenCo how it must do all of that to be successful. And in the case of GreenCo, politics play a role—what if GreenCo doesn't consider the impact of various environmental legislative initiatives on its business? How would these various initiatives affect the company's ability to sell products?

Once finalized, rules determined through modeling need to be documented. And if they change, the new rules need to be propagated throughout the organization so everyone knows they've changed.

Goals and Objectives

Once GreenCo is satisfied that its strategy is feasible, it must organize and task its employees to deliver on the strategy. GreenCo might start by setting a goal of 10 percent penetration of the addressable market with a series of efficient, low-cost units for the average homeowner. Specific goals and objectives will touch multiple functions, including R&D, manufacturing, sales, and marketing.

Commitment with Planning

Planning is the process that connects goals and objectives to execution by operationalizing them and setting specific numerical goals for each functions. For example, GreenCo's sales and marketing must develop campaigns to create awareness and generate sales leads. Based on resources and channel capacity, specific sales targets must be set, and expense, revenue, and profit plans developed. Once this demand planning has been completed, manufacturing and supply chain planning must be accomplished—with specific materials and production and distribution plans developed. And, finally, R&D must plan to deliver a series of increasingly advanced devices to satisfy changing or growing market demands, should all the other plans prove out.

Put another way, plans are what an organization commits to do in support of its objectives. Plans are the system of record of assumptions about its business and of what it has decided it is actually going to do. Without plans, there are no commitments. And without commitments, there is no accountability.

Execution

This is the phase where GreenCo will test and realize its goals and objectives. This is also where key learnings take place and where GreenCo can test its assumptions about the market, its own abilities and competition, and so on.

Tracking with Reporting and Monitoring

In between execution and evaluation activities are the measurement, monitoring, and reporting processes that will tell GreenCo whether it is attaining the expected outcomes based on the plan of record for the business. If GreenCo discovers that something is not working, the company can make decisions to reallocate resources and alter tactics to better execute the plan.

These processes sit on top of the operational data, whether the data is in a data warehouse or not, and are a formal way of observing a business. Remember the candy store analogy? In the single-proprietor candy store, all of this observation is done by one person with his own eyes. In the large, modern organization, these observations are made by many people and many systems, including transactional systems such as ERP. When made by transactional systems, the observations consist of data locked away in those systems. Reporting applications tap into this data in a useful way.

Evaluation

Here we take stock and determine whether we have achieved our goals. Were GreenCo's strategy and ability to execute up to par? Which aspects of GreenCo's strategy worked and which did not? Where did the company experience operational issues? Which processes were most or least efficient?

Perspective with Analytics
Once GreenCo has evaluated its performance and determined where it was successful and unsuccessful, it must begin an analytical process to study the results in a more in-depth fashion to determine causal factors, changes to the environment that were not expected, and possible future outcomes. Based on the outcome of this process, GreenCo must feed its new understanding of the market and its capabilities back into the vision and strategy activity to better optimize it and align it with the real world.

All of these management activities and processes occur simultaneously and not necessarily in this order. Each piece informs the next, iteration is ongoing, and many sub-processes support each step. But this simplified model is useful in clarifying the key components of a management system, no matter the size or focus of an organization.

~ 3 ~

The Role of EPM

Enterprise Performance Management is a relatively new term that refers to a processcentric, holistic approach to improving the capability of a business to gain insight and manage its performance at all levels.

The seeds of EPM were present 20 years ago in Decision Support Systems (DSS), which consisted of business analytics presented in a format appropriate for use by executives in making decisions. The strengths of DSS were also its weaknesses—these tools were created by highly trained users for use primarily by a select group of elite users and limited to large enterprises.

DSS solutions also were limited to expensive and complex statistical analysis or standard reporting packages—typically on 132-column green-bar paper. Spreadsheets were becoming more popular, but were not connected to corporate data. To analyze corporate data, users had to re-enter that data from hardcopy reports into spreadsheets—a time-consuming and error-prone process. Executive Information systems (EIS) were on the horizon, promising to deliver "high touch" applications for executives to analyze data.

Since the days when "cut-and-paste" was cutting edge, business analytics have made huge strides, evolving into what we now know as BI. Today, BI tools and technologies have become more usable, functional, and scalable. Standardization around Web interfaces and Data Manipulation Languages (DML) have simplified their implementation and use.

However, in spite of this, the overall penetration of BI remains relatively low. Even in well-established markets, like North America and Western Europe, less than one quarter of potential users have been automated with BI solutions. Why is this? There are several answers, including the complexity, lack of skills of average users, and the overall cost of BI.

In addition, often when BI is established, it has been purchased by an isolated department or is being used in a tactical fashion. It may also be driven by IT, which, no matter how visionary or well intentioned, will never replace the business as the driver of business initiatives.

To illustrate my point, consider that much of the IT buying behavior in large enterprises is focused on ad hoc query and reporting tools. This has generated some very large, enterprisewide BI purchases. Often, the intent is to move users to self-service. This is a response to the myriad requests for custom reports, which has created huge backlogs within IT. While this may reduce IT costs and backlogs in the near term and initially increase user penetration, it will not deliver actionable insight to an organization. Therefore, increases in usage gradually decline as the tools' shortcomings come into focus.

Although ad hoc query and reporting may be in the spotlight today, the future focus of BI is elsewhere. An increasing number of organizations are approaching BI as part of EPM. The integration of BI with EPM gives BI real purpose and makes it infinitely more actionable. It also gives query and reporting tools—used in conjunction—more of a context for detailed analysis.

The reason this transformation is important is that the goal of BI is to provide insight, while the goal of EPM is to link the insight provided by BI to the planning and control cycles of the enterprise, which deliver tangible action and, consequently, business value. This difference in the way information is used to drive business change is defining the next generation of business innovators and leaders.

To further illustrate the importance of this transformation, consider that with BI there is no direct link between a report or a dashboard that identifies an emerging issue and the systems a decision maker would use to carry out an appropriate response. For example, if a report reveals that a given hotel within a global chain is experiencing low occupancy rates, someone has to view the report, recognize the importance of that data point, and notify another individual who is empowered to act on that information. That person then must create and execute a suitable response using the appropriate financial and/or operational systems.

These multiple steps introduce latency and potential human error into what should be a fast-response process. Even worse, as the players move from system to system, the integrity of the underlying data may be compromised, resulting in the very real risk of losing sight of the essential data analysis or trend.

In contrast, with EPM, the insights coming out of BI and the responses to it are tightly linked. In our example of a global hotel chain, if a BI system indicates that hot weather causes low occupancy rates in Montana, then the response of seasonally adjusting prices to rebalance occupancy can be automatically initiated and flagged for approval by the appropriate manager. This automated process accelerates response and virtually eliminates the risk of a missed handoff. It also allows the connection between information discovery and the corresponding action to be automatically and electronically documented, so that the entire information chain becomes fully auditable. This takes transparency to an entirely new level.

Similar examples are easy to envision. A supply chain might have inherent inefficiencies. Using BI, one might discover that a key supplier is unable to deliver a certain component as quickly as the marketplace demands. EPM tells us the overall impact and allows us to model alternatives and select the best options.

Similarly, a customer database might hold great insights into purchasing patterns. BI can establish that a particular product is underperforming in a given region. But EPM can deliver the distribution, pricing, and packaging changes necessary to optimize revenue and profitability.

As organizations have become much more aware of the power of timely, relevant, and actionable insight, EPM is fast becoming a topic of discussion in conference rooms all over the world—in concept if not in name. For example, it is not difficult today to have a discussion with most executives and managers about planning, Balanced Scorecards, dashboards, or predictive modeling—something that could not have happened 20 years ago.

Much of the appeal of EPM exists because it offers a way to strategically improve the quality of management information and process, and therefore grow an organization from a collection of loosely coupled business units into the highly coordinated and agile enterprise that is necessary to succeed in today's global markets.

For example, EPM closes what I call "the fact gap," which is a lack of factual information or real understanding of an organization's performance during decision making. In a fact gap, organizations make decisions using outdated information, borrowed perspectives, and sometimes even pure guesswork.

There are two categories of fact gaps—operational, which affects the measurement of efficiency, and market-focused, which affects customer leverage and market opportunities. Left unchecked, fact gaps have the potential to cause business initiatives or even entire businesses to fail.

EPM also delivers management information in a timely way and hosts management processes in a single, interactive, and collaborative environment. This allows teams of managers across the enterprise and the extended enterprise to collectively plan, measure performance, anticipate results, and drive profitability.

And EPM can play a crucial role in helping an organization manage its relationships in a decentralized business network. Using EPM, organizations can plan and measure together with its partners and adjust accordingly. This can be done daily, weekly, monthly, or in whatever timeframes make sense. It can also help foster collaboration and trust by facilitating shared goal setting and providing access to information that helps all parties monitor and confirm mutual success. In a decentralized business network, objective data is often the best arbitrator.

EPM AND PLANNING

Perhaps nowhere is the impact of EPM felt more dramatically than in the enterprise planning process. This is because advances in planning practices are largely dependent on advances in planning technology. EPM can transform planning from an annual exercise that adds little value to an organization to one that ensures the continuous optimization of resource allocation decisions and consistent, effective execution of business strategy across an enterprise.

As is the case with all important management processes, enterprise planning and the tools that support it have continually evolved together over time. Before computers, companies performed planning tasks with paper spreadsheets and calculators. The introduction of PCs and desktop spreadsheets made planning faster, offered opportunities for great flexibility, and made it easier to share and update planning documents.

Spreadsheet programs were later enhanced with specialized budgeting applications, and then more recently, the Internet and Web-based applications provided browser-based access to shared planning databases and documents. This meant that planning documents could be maintained on central servers rather than being stored on multiple individual users' desktops.

Both of these innovations—specialized applications and Web-enabled applications—made enormous contributions to the effectiveness of the enterprise planning process. Specialized programs enabled businesses to more quickly and reliably build planning documents based on more sophisticated models. And Web-enabled applications solved the problems of version control and auditing because planning documents could then be stored centrally. But neither advance did much—if anything—to introduce dynamism and collaboration into what was still largely a static, top-down process. The advance that was required to make that happen was EPM.

Among the improvements EPM can make to the enterprise planning process:

Unified Planning

There are a multitude of financial and operational plans, budgets, and forecasts in any organization, including strategic and operating plans, outlooks and scenarios, revenue, expense and cash flow forecasts, capital expenditure and workforce plans, and marketing, sales, and administrative budgets.

EPM brings these separate planning processes together.

Dynamic, Real-Time Updates

Business today moves too quickly for organizations to rely on annual or quarterly numbers alone. Allocation decisions and forecast revisions have to be made based on conditions that can change at any time.

EPM facilitates the ability to adjust more frequently—or even continuously—by providing automated, Web-based links to planning drivers across the enterprise. As a result, events or initiatives in one part of the organization can drive rapid responses in other parts of the organization. This dynamic approach eliminates the lag times and disconnects associated with conventional planning tools and the annual or quarterly planning process.

Multitiered Aggregation and Granularity

Planning takes place on many levels, from the boardroom to the front lines. But if each level uses a separate planning system, aggregating plans becomes a difficult and time-consuming process. Even worse, it can be virtually impossible for top management to drill down from an aggregated document to discover underlying issues at the desired level of granularity. In addition, the manual aggregation of multiple spreadsheets introduces the possibility of error.

EPM solves these issues by unifying all planning systems into a single planning environment in which all data is appropriately linked vertically across all organizational levels and horizontally across all departments and functions.

Integration with Enterprise Application and Data Sources

Planning and budgeting are affected by a diverse range of environmental factors: sales pipelines, burdened labor rates, cost of materials, interest rates, currency exchange rates, and so on. This data is typically stored in ERP systems, HR applications, external information services, and other internal sources. It makes good sense to tap into these sources to dynamically adjust planning variables to reflect changing conditions.

EPM provides the integration interfaces and variable adjustment functions necessary to do this. And, because planners often want to work with such data with familiar tools, EPM also provides interfaces to such familiar tools as Microsoft Office.

Translation between Financial and Operational Metrics

One of the keys to good planning is collaboration of all appropriate people across the enterprise. A Web-based application fosters collaboration by facilitating the distribution of functionality anywhere and everywhere it's needed. However, it's just as important to facilitate collaboration between business users—who think and act primarily in terms of business operations—and finance users—who typically drive planning processes using budgets.

EPM facilitates collaboration between finance and operations by providing automated translations between financial and nonfinancial metrics such as headcount, materials, and product units.

Enhanced Creation and Management of "What-If" Models

A big part of planning is the modeling and assessing of multiple, divergent scenarios. What if we add more regional facilities? What if interest rates rise dramatically? What if sales misses its quarterly goal by 10 percent? Managers must continually ask these types of questions and accurately gauge their implications. Spreadsheets make it difficult to work with multiple theoretical scenarios—especially since they lack tools for linking related scenarios to one another in meaningful ways.

EPM allows multiple alternative scenarios to be managed in a common manner, allowing decision makers across an organization to freely experiment with various hypo-thetical conditions without creating document chaos in the process or undermining the integrity of the core planning documents.

Of course, technology alone has little value; it requires that organizations apply it in the right way by using it to support best practices. In the case of the enterprise planning process, using EPM to support best practices in planning results in the following benefits:

- Faster, more appropriate response to change by reducing planning cycle times
- Actionable insight at users' fingertips by making all planning data across the enterprise available in a single, easy-to-use application
- Predictable performance by enabling continual assessment of real performance versus projected results and maintaining alignment between projections and execution
- Optimal allocation of resources by linking planning across the enterprise based on logical dependencies
- Full enfranchisement and unity of direction across the enterprise by ensuring that everyone at every level works together to achieve common goals
- Clearer vision, greater creativity, and stronger leadership by enabling an organization to examine multiple what-if scenarios
- More confidence in planning and forecasting by using a disciplined approach

PLANNING AS A DRIVER OF PROCESS CHANGE

As an example of an organization using EPM to implement planning best practices, consider this major U.S. university.

An early adopter of EPM for operational analysis, the university decided in 2007 to extend its use of EPM to planning and budgeting functions. The goal is to gain more accurate insight into both its financial and operational data, enabling more reliable plans and forecasts and more insightful analysis of ongoing operations.

Specifically, this university wants to give its financial analysts access to a centralized performance management system that provides an in-depth look at university operations and their related impact on financials by tightly integrating financial and operational planning models. Once in place, the new system will enable the university's fiscal managers in central university offices, individual schools, and business units to generate reports to keep university administrators current on the status of key business processes affecting every member of the community.

To accomplish this, the system will tap into the university's data warehouse, which contains information directly from the university's student information system and various financial systems. With the system's reporting tools, university staff members can then access an intuitive and highly interactive interface to design their own dashboards for monitoring status and drilling down on relevant information.

By integrating management, planning, and modeling for various financial and business applications into a single system, the university will have reports that are drawn from the same consistent set of information and a unified view of its financial and operational data whenever its needs it.

Another example of an organization using EPM to drive process change—specifically to unify its planning and forecasting processes—is a U.S.-based leader in security software. The company has operations in more than dozens of countries and employs more than 15,000 people.

The challenge of unifying planning and forecasting at the company was made more complex by the company's fast growth through a series of acquisitions. Each new acquisition brought new systems for functions such as reporting, planning, and financial consolidation. Because each department had one or more of its own systems for managing these functions, the business planning process involved financial analysts interviewing each budget manager individually to obtain forecast and budget data. The analysts would then rekey this data into a homegrown tool or spreadsheet. As the company grew to more than 6,000 cost centers, completing a forecast cycle typically took each analyst a solid month's work.

In addition, discrepancies in how product data was captured by different business units made it difficult to produce accurate rollup information to analyze product sales consistently.

In implementing EPM, the company's top priority was to find an integrated platform that would be accessible to all employees. In addition to automating the planning process, the company wanted to add more accountability to the process by having business unit managers be responsible for entering their own information into the system.

After selecting its EPM solution in 2003, the planning process took about four weeks for system design and another month for testing and refining. Training sessions were held in stages for the 800 users of the system. Deployments of subsequent components of the system were completed within an average time of three months.

With EPM, the company has streamlined its planning process and enabled more people to actively participate while reducing the time it takes to gather and analyze the underlying data. As a result, even though the company has doubled in size in the past few years, it has increased its ability to react to business change by having a more accurate and accessible view of business conditions available to more people in the organization.

One more example is a U.S. firm that provides homes for nearly 10,000 seniors and uses EPM to streamline its planning processes and plan for future growth. With senior campuses in six states, the firm plans aggressive expansion over the next five years. One of the biggest challenges associated with its expansion plans was budgeting—a problem that no longer exists since the company implemented EPM.

Prior to EPM, the company was unable to give its 300 business managers in various locations direct access to its ERP system to create their own budgets. Therefore, the firm identified as its primary need the ability to keep standardized forms and reports in a centralized location, yet be able to distribute them on the Web to a large number of users. The company also needed the ability to modify and retrieve collected data and create a standard package of reports. Since implementing EPM, budgeting at the firm has, in the words of one executive, gone from "a nightmare to a nonissue."

The firm also will use EPM to forecast labor and construction costs for new campuses. Its goal is to have 30 communities within the next five years, a growth of six times its current size, and so careful planning is essential to ensure this growth is profitable. Each campus is built one at a time, and construction takes about three to five years.

Forecasting labor and construction costs will consist of entering the expenses from every phase of a job—from the cost of dry wall to on-site labor—into a general ledger system. With this information, the company will be able to find variances within the budget, compare one job to another, and create standards for future jobs.

Today, EPM also simplifies the firm's entire financial management process, helping managers focus their efforts on budget analysis, planning, modeling, and forecasting instead of the data entry and collection mechanics.

This company demonstrates how EPM takes finance to a new level—helping managers create accurate financial plans to achieve company goals, while cutting costs and, therefore, increasing profits.

EPM AND COMPLIANCE

Another area in which EPM has had an enormous impact is in compliance with financial and other regulations that affect businesses and business reporting. While many of the headlines have been reserved for new financial regulations, other laws such as the Health Insurance Portability and Accountability Act (HIPAA), designed to improve health care access and prevent health care fraud and abuse in the United States, and the Patriot Act, which gives the U.S. government access to business information previously considered confidential, have raised the bar on compliance as well.

In particular, stringent new corporate accounting and reporting rules have surfaced in recent years as governments all over the world have responded to the crisis of confidence in business that arose in the wake of Enron and other high-profile corporate cases in the early 2000s. In the United States, for example, based on recommendations from the Securities & Exchange Commission (SEC) and public pressure, a massive corporate reform measure known as the Sarbanes-Oxley Act became law in 2002.

The Sarbanes-Oxley Act demands more auditing insight and requires CEOs and CFOs to personally certify their companies' financial results or suffer severe civil and criminal penalties.

Similarly, the European Union (EU) parliament endorsed a proposal that requires all EU companies listed on a regulated market to prepare and publish their consolidated accounts in accordance with a single set of International Accounting Standards (IAS), also known as International Financial Reporting Standards (IFRS). The aim of standardizing the reporting of results was to make financial results more comparable, thereby making the European capital market more efficient. Without standardized reporting—even if all other barriers to efficiency are removed—investors likely will remain skeptical and demand a premium for their capital.

By any yardstick, regulations such as the Sarbanes-Oxley Act of 2002 and IAS/IFRS 2005 are extraordinary measures that pose extraordinary challenges for companies affected by them. In the United States, adequate integrated financial management systems and internal controls are no longer nice to have: they are the law under Sarbanes-Oxley. In addition, credibility is paramount and must be demonstrated by faster reporting cycles, full disclosure, and no restatements.

These regulations—and the very real personal liability they created—have caused changes from the boardroom to the mailroom as boards of directors and management teams had to rethink how their companies plan, measure, and report performance. The goal was to find and implement solutions that would enable them to report openly and comprehensively on their performance with confidence.

Purposeful violations aside, many companies legitimately struggle to gather, understand, and report financial information. Because financial information is often siloed in transactional systems or locked in spreadsheets, it can be extremely difficult if not impossible to create a single reliable, accurate, and complete view of a company's performance. The problem is compounded in large companies with numerous individual, geographically dispersed, operating units, many of which likely use transactional systems from different vendors.

Specifically when it comes to reporting, however, another problem is that many companies lack a single reporting infrastructure that enables managers to create comprehensive management-oriented reports for internal use and to generate reports for external use that comply with statutory reporting requirements and other needs of external stakeholders. This disconnect between reports for internal and external use adds to the difficulty of creating a single version of the truth about a company's financial performance.

As companies that have implemented EPM are discovering, EPM can play a crucial role in addressing this disconnect by providing a single view of the company's performance that includes both financial and operational information integrated into a single reporting structure. This idea—that compliance and performance are linked—is very much in the spirit of Sarbanes-Oxley, IAS/IFRS 2005, and other regulatory reforms. Whatever their merits or shortcomings, these reforms are intended to restore public trust in corporations' ability to produce shareholder value. That spirit is as much about performance and accountability as it is about compliance.

To illustrate this point, think of a company that has difficulty putting together its income statement and balance sheet each quarter or knowing within 48 hours when a material event has happened. Is this really a company that can consistently produce a profit quarter after quarter, year after year? How would the executives know for sure that the company did in fact operate profitably over the long haul if it has a hard time arriving at its numbers today?

Conversely, think of a well-run company that understands and tracks its key performance indicators (KPIs)—whatever they may be—a company that knows which products, customers, regions, and production plants are most profitable and does a good job of monitoring cash flow. This company will find it much easier to become compliant.

With an understanding that more substantial benefits come from greater visibility into your business and with it, the ability to make mid-course corrections to improve performance—cutting costs in difficult times and investing in more robust times—the question is, how can you move your organization beyond compliance to breakthrough performance?

The answer, of course, is EPM.

LEVERAGING COMPLIANCE TO IMPROVE PERFORMANCE

A European financial services provider is an example of a company that uses EPM to achieve both compliance and better performance. As a fully licensed bank, the company is subject to the changing solvency requirements in the banking industry.

Specifically, banks are currently required to reserve 8 percent of issued loans to absorb losses, but from 2007 onward, they will be allowed to diversify their risks to a great extent. These arrangements were agreed to in new regulations known in banking circles as Basel II.

This particular company's response to Basel II, IFRS, and other changing international regulation was to leverage its short-term requirement of compliance into a long-term commitment to more sophisticated techniques for monitoring and improving performance. These include economic capital (EC) modeling, risk adjusted return on capital (RAROC) modeling—for which IFRS provides the required calculation methods—and value-based management (VBM), which is a comprehensive set of activities that maximize value.

The company had earlier implemented EPM for budgeting, which enabled it to more easily produce reports required under Basel II and RAROC requirements. The company is currently implementing an EPM system that will further enable it to establish links that will let its various EPM applications share data and metadata. This will yield data and knowledge that will determine the desired shareholders' equity on every deal the company does. These and other changes are bringing the company closer to VBM, a major change from a strategy geared more toward financial control and book profits to one that is more focused on strategic control and value.

One of the largest electronics retailers in the United States is another example of a company that leveraged compliance into performance management. Its primary motivation in adopting EPM was to solve the problem of a frustrating disconnect between information required by management to run the company and information needed for external reporting.

As recently as 2002, the firm suffered from a decentralized budgeting and reporting process and inconsistency in how each company group did its budgeting and reporting. Similar to other large, decentralized companies, the firm had some groups with a manufacturing focus, others with a retail focus, and no alignment between how groups reported performance internally and how it needed to report externally.

The company's issues were heightened by its use of a spreadsheet-based budgeting system. This meant that headquarters was routinely receiving budgets from 12 different entities without much visibility into how those budgets were being created. In addition to a lack of visibility and common processes, the company lacked a clear company-wide goal in its budgeting process.

When the firm decided to tackle the problem, the company included in its defined requirements a need for top-level visibility into all budget details; better communication at all levels regarding current budget numbers and issues; a uniform income statement hierarchy for all reporting units; easy-to-use reporting tools; and a means to incorporate current financial reporting data into budgeting systems.

To meet these requirements, the firm combined EPM planning and reporting software to pull company financial data from existing applications and to enable collaborative budgeting and forecasting throughout the company. Groups now prepare a standard set of monthly financial reports, and are free to create their own ad hoc reports. Most important, all reports—whether corporatewide or ad hoc for a group, whether internal or external—are all driven by a single version of the truth about the company's performance.

HOW EPM WORKS FROM A USER'S PERSPECTIVE

Up to now, the real-world examples of EPM I have cited have focused on process changes and benefits to organizations. But to understand how EPM improves the working styles of individual users, consider this before-and-after scenario.

Before EPM, a manager might get a report or spreadsheet indicating a variance from plan. To better understand details/causal factors, he or she would have to access multiple application or reporting systems—all with different views and perspectives on the data. These different perspectives then would have to be manually reconciled (using spreadsheets and cut-and-paste) and then compared to the plan of record—another spreadsheet typically held by the finance department. Any changes to the plans would have to be authorized and made by finance. The new plan of record would then be emailed to all of management with an explanation for the changes.

Multiply this process by the number of managers in any organization and it becomes clear how problematic it is.

In contrast, with a modern EPM system, a manager is presented with a scorecard or dashboard displaying metrics that are relevant to his or her performance. Variances can easily be seen and explained by examining the information, from all perspectives, to fully comprehend what occurred and why. Any required changes to plan are made by the manager and approved in the same system and without having to populate and email spreadsheets. Annotations are made to the plan so other managers can understand the rationale for the changes.

Here is an even more specific scenario. Suppose you were a regional vice president of a bank, and when viewing your dashboard, you noticed an unfavorable variance in net income for one of your branches. Using conventional tools, you'd have to jump through an endless web of hyperlinked reports, or drill through multiple layers of data, or sift through reports in a repository. More likely, you'd call someone and have him or her do it for you.

But imagine if you could just type in a few key words in a search bar and be immediately presented with a set of relevant business topics related to net income and drivers of profitability. And for any one of those topics—product profitability, for example—the system presented you with predefined questions in your native language. And then gave you the ability to refine the question to get the specific answer you wanted.

And if you then wanted to change the time period for your inquiry from a quarterly view to a year-to-date view, making that change would just be a matter of clicking on the time period and selecting your alternative.

But what if you were interested in understanding what's behind those numbers? Where would you start?

EPM would help guide you along that path. For example, you could mouse over the gross profit metric for a particular product and be presented with a menu of relevant metrics that relate to or drive gross profit, such as marketing expenses, growth rate, or plan variance for that product area.

Another way in which EPM would help you is through adaptive visualization. If you've used Amazon, you're familiar with how the system remembers your past experiences on the site and adapts that historical memory to your current interactions, presenting information and suggestions that are of direct relevance to you at that moment in time. Adaptive visualization is one capability required to make this work.

The fact is that people like to view information in different ways, depending on individual preferences, the type of information, and its business context. Using adaptive visualization, EPM would automatically select the most optimal views of information based on your history, preferences, and the nature of the data.

For example, if you were to add additional KPIs to the report described earlier, the tables presenting the data would become much more complex. So, wouldn't it be nice if, upon selecting those additional performance indicators, EPM automatically changed your view from a table to a bubble chart that used color, size, spatial placement, and annotations to make it easier to immediately understand?

Another area of emerging focus for EPM is decision management. Have you ever encountered a situation in business where a decision was made, acted upon, and then, after the fact (either because it turned out to be a great decision or a horrible decision), no one could remember how the decision was made in the first place? EPM should be able to record the decision-making process, making it easier to audit how and why business decisions are made, ultimately so that best practices can be captured and embedded into future behavior.

Much of what I've discussed in this example focuses on the business user, but the burden of making EPM successful ultimately rests on the shoulders of IT. It's hard, especially when things change on a daily basis. Reports change, applications change, source systems change, processes change, and organizational structures change. And at the end of the day, guess who has to implement those changes in the system? That's why EPM must also focus on liberating IT from the complexities of development, deployment, and management.

One example of a EPM capability for IT would be an environment for authoring and application development that provides a layer of abstraction that presents technical information in business terms. This would insulate report authors and application developers from having to understand source system data models, structures, and query languages. Such an environment would also make it easier to create and manage applications in a way that recognizes relationships between entities and manage the flow of both data and metadata between applications.

For instance, if you were an application developer for a bank, you could develop a branch-level budget model that contains a much greater level of granularity than that which is used at the regional or corporate level. You could start with an aerial view of all applications and models that share common dimensions, hierarchies, metadata, and master data. You could model the flow of data and metadata between applications. When new applications or revisions are put in production, you could ensure that everything is synchronized within the applications, and that all changes to master data are propagated to external systems that share dimensions and hierarchies.

At its core, EPM is the quintessential planning tool for the business, ultimately enabling individuals to determine what they do next. It exposes issues that will influence performance, ensures process and exploration that supports collective decision making, and allows for mistakes and course correction.

DRIVERS OF EPM ADOPTION

As the powerful capabilities of EPM become better known, many organizations are implementing EPM initiatives that target certain aspects of performance management or are departmental in scope as a way of preparing for enterprisewide EPM initiatives. These organizations typically are motivated by a combination of external and internal pressures, many of which I have already discussed.

Regardless of their motivation, businesses today recognize that the keys to success go beyond the ability to track and understand past performance. Businesses today must understand performance drivers well enough to plan and execute against future goals.

EPM initiatives today take many forms. Here is an example of one company and its motivation for adopting EPM.

Modeling as the Key to a Successful Growth Strategy

A diversified industrial technology and services company based in Europe is using EPM and especially strategic modeling to support a divestment and growth strategy. The company was already using EPM for planning and reporting, but early on, the company also decided it wanted to put in place processes and systems that would enable it to do a better job of understanding the impact of its strategic corporate decisions before they are made.

As with other businesses with operations all over the world, the company now has new regulatory requirements to meet. Not only must it report its results under General Acceptable Accounting Principles (GAAP), it must also meet new and more stringent reporting requirements dictated by the EU, including IFRS.

The company decided to first tackle the challenges it was facing in the area of financial consolidations, which were very similar to many other large companies with operating units around the world. As financial consolidations became more difficult, they had begun to affect the company's planning and budgeting processes, making them less efficient, too.

The company was using a specialized application for financial consolidations at its headquarters, but its 60 operating companies submitted their data using spreadsheets and it was taking six weeks to consolidate that many different versions of the "truth." By optimizing processes, the company managed to cut its reporting cycle to two weeks. However, the company wanted to further streamline the consolidation process and be able to access one central source of data. That would take technology.

To unite its far-flung strategic units and further reduce reporting cycles, the company implemented an EPM financial management application at its headquarters, which took about three months. Within a few more months, all of the company's operating companies were using the same application. An important feature of the application was that it allowed the company's regional business units to input their data according to local accounting practices and standards, which were then easily translated into corporate standards.

One important result was one version of the truth across all areas of the company, which enabled the company to make better operational decisions and improve efficiencies and profitability.

Equally important, the company shortened its reporting time by another week and decreased its throughput times from weeks to hours. A typical closing process now unfolds something like this: Operating companies have their data in by 1 P.M. on the appointed day. The company has its results to the board of directors by 4 P.M. By the end of the day, management has full visibility into current and historic financial results.

With these process and systems improvements, the company was able to reduce the number of people required to perform financial consolidations from 14 to 3. This enabled the company to redeploy nine people to higher value added tasks such as analysis.

With consolidation and reporting well in hand, the company turned its attention to understanding its KPIs as a precursor to improving performance.

Before EPM, the company's business units were unable to access financial data used at headquarters. As a result, meetings often started with lengthy discussions about the data, leaving less time for discussions about important strategic decisions. The company needed a way for all local, regional, and strategic unit controllers to see the data, approve the data, and send it to higher levels in the company. It also needed a database that would contain all management information so that in discussions with the board of directors, everyone could start with the same data.

To meet this challenge, the company created key performance indicator sheets with specific financial and operational performance metrics delivered via dashboards and accessible over the Web to board members and executives. This provided an up-to-date overview of the company's performance and enabled everyone at the company to work with the same data and easily analyze the data from various perspectives.

The next step for the company was to look for a solution to the problem of accurately forecasting the financial impact of potential acquisitions and other corporate decisions. This involved analyzing the consolidated income statement, balance sheet, and cash flow impact of critical business decisions and running scenarios to evaluate the financial impact of corporate restructuring or other portfolio strategies.

To accomplish this, the company implemented an EPM strategic modeling application that could measure the potential effects of potential acquisitions on earnings accretion or dilution, debt covenants, and other key metrics.

The application had a significant impact on the company's understanding of the way financial decisions might affect the company. For example, it now is able to examine both financial and nonfinancial economic drivers of its business and align the entire company behind the strategic plan. It also can simultaneously evaluate financing and operating alternatives, such as predicting synthetic debt ratings over time, when evaluating various operating scenarios and assumptions.

A BROAD RANGE OF MOTIVATIONS

Here are some additional examples of the many reasons why organizations today are implementing EPM.

A large U.S. bank used EPM to bring common processes and systems to its business and consumer divisions, which were using similar data but different systems and methodologies for measuring performance. The differences made it difficult for senior management to gain actionable insight into companywide productivity and other KPIs.

To resolve these differences, the bank decided to create a performance scorecarding application that would enable it to measure performance for both businesses in a meaningful yet comparable way. The application also needed to be flexible enough to allow quarterly changes to performance metrics, if necessary, and a robust reporting and analysis capability that would enable senior management to drill down for a better understanding of performance drivers.

The first step toward building such an application was to modify the corporate data warehouse to provide 95 percent of all data needed for the creation of scorecards. Then, the bank chose a BI platform solution to store business rules and historical data for its scorecards and to provide analytical drill-down capabilities. A reporting application helps analysts create PDF reports that are distributed over the Web. Today, performance scorecards applications are used by thousands of people at the bank.

The U.S. subsidiary of a large semiconductor manufacturer implemented EPM to track and quantify customer profitability so it could do a better job of allocating resources to more profitable customers. Using existing applications it had developed using a BI platform and development tools, the company built an application for top management, sales, and finance that gives them insight into the current profitability and the ability to forecast the future profitability of each customer. It also enables users to perform sensitive "what-if" analyses of customers to determine potential outcomes of changes in resource allocations.

A leading financial services company turned to EPM out of a desire to deploy an enterprisewide profitability reporting solution. The overarching goal was to answer the basic question, "How are our various products really contributing to the bottom line?"

The firm decided that creating such a solution would require a streamlined, standardized, and centralized system capable of measuring the profitability of product teams, investment teams, and distribution channels. The firm formed a project team to define requirements and make recommendations to top management, and then to develop and automate new processes. New processes included common cost allocation methods, drivers, and hierarchies across business units. The firm chose an allocation, consolidation, and reporting engine upon which to base its firmwide solution and then built and implemented a system that emphasized user control so it could be used with a minimum of IT involvement.

The system today delivers detailed P&Ls across all product lines with a significantly reduced cycle time, implements nightly iteration cycles, has improved productivity by reducing 75 percent of nonvalue added process steps, creates detailed audit trails, and has flattened learning curves for analysts throughout the firm.

A leading technology consulting firm implemented EPM—and specifically an online management performance reporting tool—to reduce the time it was taking to distribute performance management reports to its partners. The firm reached this conclusion after a firmwide survey of partners and principals revealed that 80 percent believed online access to performance reports would improve their ability to manage the business. The firm also wanted to put a stop to a fragmented yet growing rogue effort in the firm that resulted in 60 to 80 analysts working full-time on generating ad hoc performance reports that varied from analyst to analyst and lacked a single version of the truth.

To create such a system, which the firm calls an "EPM portal," the firm used a BI platform and EPM applications for reporting and planning. The system took about nine months to build and reduced the time it takes to distribute performance reports from 15 days to less than 5 days following the close of books.

A large U.S. retailer in an extremely competitive business has implemented several EPM projects to date, starting with the goal of making better financial decisions, but quickly moving to performance management as a key to operational excellence. Early on, the company decided that the key to operational excellence is to have accurate, timely, and detailed information about the performance of each individual store, the factors that influence its performance, and how the performance of that store affects the company overall. The company was especially interested in the KPIs that drive gross margin, including inventory levels across the country; which products have the highest margins; and whether inventory is sufficient to meet customer demand.

The company also wanted to focus on key indicators that improve productivity and efficiency, such as which products are selling best in which region and the effectiveness of specific marketing and advertising campaigns.

Having this kind of detailed operational information on a daily basis provides insight that allows the company to make daily decisions about how to improve performance—at the store level, at the regional level, or companywide. And that depends on two things: technology, and processes that support sophisticated planning, forecasting, and decision making.

To meet this challenge, the company turned to a BI platform that combined data integration, OLAP, query and reporting, ad hoc analysis, and application development tools to support informed and proactive decision making.

The company now provides Web-based daily sales and other important financial information by major segments and stores to each of its district locations. Each district reviews its business daily and compares it to previous levels and to forecasts and goals. More important, districts can make immediate midcourse corrections or improvements using best practices learned from their peers—information about operational successes and failure points—making its analytics actionable.

TOWARD GREATER ACCOUNTABILITY

As these examples illustrate, EPM today is well equipped to tackle many of the day-to-day barriers to effective performance management. But it also has the capability to achieve a more fundamental and lasting benefit. EPM can help organizations achieve greater accountability, a state in which individuals at all levels work collaboratively toward shared objectives, striving for breakthrough performance and accountability in all their actions. Organizations also begin to manage beyond isolated functions and can understand impact across the enterprise.

A key success factor in building a performance-accountable organization is a commitment to increasing each person's knowledge and understanding of what drives performance in that organization. What is the potential impact of a planned acquisition on the balance sheet? Can existing inventory cover the forecast? How do current sales compare to forecasts and forecasts to plans? How will a change in marketing programs affect sales and production and vice versa? Insight into these questions and others is necessary for individuals to see the big picture and understand the impact of their actions on the rest of the organization.

Only top management that embraces the concept of transparency can deliver these kinds of insights broadly to people throughout their organizations. In their 2003 book, *The Naked Corporation*, Don Tapscott and David Ticoll wrote that we are in an age of transparency that will revolutionize business. They defined transparency as going beyond the obligation to disclose financial information to offering all stakeholders who interact with a company unprecedented visibility into the performance, operations, behavior, and values of the company. Because stakeholders have at their fingertips the most powerful tools ever for finding out, informing others, and self-organizing, the corporation is becoming naked.

Tapscott and Ticoll argue that becoming naked is not a bad thing, but it's not necessarily an easy state in which to live. For example, if you're going to be naked, fitness is no longer an option because nothing is hidden from view. You must be buff. An organization that says it offers the best value had better do so. An organization offering a commodity product had better have the best price, and one not in a commodity market had better have differentiated value.

Equally important, organizations need to have values and live up to them because without integrity there is no trust. The smart organizations understand that rather than something to be feared, transparency is a force that can be harnessed for growth, success, and sustainability.

An important note: Tapscott and Ticoll believe that every company needs a transparency strategy and say they were amazed when they were doing their research for the book that few companies have one and that most are just "winging it." The danger of winging it is that someone in one department releases some information and someone in another department may release contradictory information. This type of conflict can result in all kinds of unintended consequences.

The authors recommend that organizations stand back and look at how their various stakeholders use or could benefit from information. What are the risks and vulnerabilities? What are the potential payoffs and benefits? After this kind of evaluation, organizations can develop a comprehensive approach to transparency.

Another success factor is a commitment to developing the connective management processes that support the four core activities of a management cycle discussed in a previous chapter: vision and strategy supported by rationalization, goal and objective setting supported by commitment, execution supported by tracking, and evaluation supported by perspective.

How each of these four core activities is done will vary depending on where the activity takes place in an organization. For example, every business produces strategic and operational plans. But a strategic business unit may plan in quite a different way from a manufacturing business unit. One unit might use metrics based on the core strategic objectives, while another might focus on metrics of volume, cost, and quality.

It is important to note that everything within an enterprise is related directly or indirectly to everything else. The same is true with metrics. Understanding these relationships and how to reconcile them is the key to strategic EPM.

Each core activity also has a number of subactivities and tasks, which also will vary by industry and business unit.

Regardless of the exact circumstances of their use, the core activities are designed to provide feedback. In this way, the entire performance management cycle can improve over time and become more effective.

Combined, these core activities enable organizations to set financial and nonfinancial goals to improve both financial and operational performance, model underlying business drivers, plan based on the drivers, establish metrics for monitoring progress, and then monitor and report performance—in other words, establish performance accountability.

An important starting place in the journey to achieve performance accountability is to understand the Nine Tenets of a Performance-Accountable Organization and how they map to core management processes.

THE NINE TENETS

A performance-accountable organization:

#1: **Finds truth in numbers.** A single version of the truth guides performance at all levels of the organization.

#2: **Sets accurate expectations.** Every part of the business is directed by a shared commitment to strategic goals.

#3: **Anticipates results.** A thorough understanding of business drivers and key performance indicators leads to an ability to anticipate results.

#4: **Plans with impact.** Insight and dynamic processes produce actionable plans that continually guide the organization to success in changing conditions.

#5: **Achieves on–demand visibility.** A system that combines data from existing transactional systems across the enterprise gives managers transparent access to performance information anytime, anywhere.

#6: **Delivers continuous improvement.** A commitment to knowledge and understanding produces insight that drives continuous performance improvement.

#7: **Reports with confidence.** Detailed, integrated, and accessible financial and operational information enables executives to personally certify business results.

#8: **Executes with conviction.** Truth, clarity, and confidence forge a powerful link between strategy, plans, and execution.

#9: **Stands up to scrutiny.** A comprehensive approach meets the highest standards of accountability and confidence.

I will revisit these Nine Tenets in more detail in Chapter 10.

~ 4 ~

Barriers to EPM Adoption

Despite the demonstrated benefits and appealing promises of EPM, as with any new technology, adoption barriers abound. I'd like to focus on two of the most common: ineffective approaches to implementing EPM initiatives, and the current state of EPM tools and technologies.

A MULTITUDE OF EPM APPROACHES

The way an organization approaches implementing EPM speaks volumes about its readiness to succeed at performance management. The organizations most ready are those that have achieved a balance in terms of the maturity of their business users and IT. Organizations with a high level of IT maturity and a low level of business user maturity tend to use an approach I call "One Size Fits All." Organizations with high business user maturity and low IT maturity use an approach I call "A Thousand Flowers Bloom."

In my view, organizations with both low business user and IT maturity are stuck in a kind of EPM "Middle Ages." And finally—and of course these are the shining stars—organizations with a high level of both IT and business user maturity enjoy a kind of EPM "Utopia."

One Size Fits All

In this approach, IT calls the shots when it comes to EPM. And typically, in its desire to achieve stability, picks one tool that is easy to manage and one centralized data warehouse with little concern for the variety of user needs and for the comprehensiveness and integration of EPM initiatives across the business. It is my strong belief that an EPM initiative driven by IT—no matter how visionary or well intentioned the IT team is—will never replace the business as the driver.

To illustrate this point, much of the IT buying behavior in large enterprises is focused on ad hoc query and reporting tools. This has generated some very large, enterprisewide purchases. And while this approach may reduce IT costs and backlog in the near term and increase user penetration initially, it will not result in substantial improvements in overall business performance because it is not comprehensive and integrated. Therefore, any increase in user penetration will be offset by a gradual decline in usage, as the tools' shortcomings come into focus.

My advice to organizations in which IT believes that one size fits all is to proceed with extreme caution.

A Thousand Flowers Bloom

In contrast, in this approach, users rule. Every line of business or even every department is allowed to pursue its own course for EPM, including selecting its own projects, tools, and methodologies. In these organizations, EPM is fragmented, solutions are siloed with little or no coordination across departments or lines of businesses, and implementations are tactical. Data marts abound, and planning, forecasting, and budgeting are typically done using disjointed spreadsheets, resulting in a kind of "spreadsheet hell."

I know of a bank with multiple fairly autonomous businesses in various geographies that uses more than 6,000 different spreadsheets in different parts of the company for monitoring and management of performance, and reporting. Imagine how time consuming (costly) and error prone (risky) any exercise that required the bank to roll up data or information in those spreadsheets into a consolidated enterprisewide view would be.

Also, in these organizations, IT resources tend to exist within lines of businesses and departments, and central IT is viewed simply as a utility and consequently given little or no input into EPM decisions.

In addition, there is little input from top management into EPM initiatives in these organizations, so links to corporate goals and strategies are practically nonexistent.

My advice to organizations in which a thousand flowers bloom is also to proceed with extreme caution.

The Middle Ages

In organizations that are in the Middle Ages of EPM, user solutions tend to be limited to inflexible reporting and data access and—as in organizations in which a thousand flowers bloom—spreadsheets are the performance management tools of choice. Use of BI tools—let alone EPM tools—is sporadic and inconsistent. In fact, there are no initiatives around EPM per se. Intuition and experience of top management drives decision making and planning, and the budgeting process is limited to a finance exercise at best and often haphazard.

To organizations in the Middle Ages of EPM, my advice is not to bother: Your chances of success are miniscule.

Other Bad Behaviors

There are a handful of other bad behaviors that may exist in organizations that don't qualify as approaches but nonetheless reflect a lack of EPM maturity:

"Misguided Self Service." When IT doesn't comprehend user needs, it often simply throws a tool over the wall with a data warehouse.

"Insight Elitism." Only top management has access to information and insight and uses it to second guess and bully managers.

"Dashboard Myopia." IT gives users dashboards without any rationale to the metrics that are presented.

In some organizations, all these behaviors are present simultaneously.

Utopia

And finally, there is EPM Utopia. In organizations at this advanced stage of EPM maturity, the business owns EPM initiatives, has a strong partnership with IT and technology, and IT exists to support business initiatives and processes. There is very likely an EPM Center of Excellence[1] that exists outside of IT and is championed by either the CFO or a line of business executive. An EPM Center of Excellence is an organization that defines, refines, documents, and promotes best practices an organization will use to deploy EPM.

The organization has probably standardized on the right number and type of EPM tools and technologies. In budgeting, planning, and other aspects of performance management, processes are enterprisewide.

Organizations that exist in a state of EPM Utopia probably don't need any advice from me; they are already moving ahead and enjoying great success.

In these organizations, EPM initiatives are driven by the business, and by a vision the business had for EPM and

---

[1]EPM Centers of Excellence are sometimes known as EPM Competency Centers.

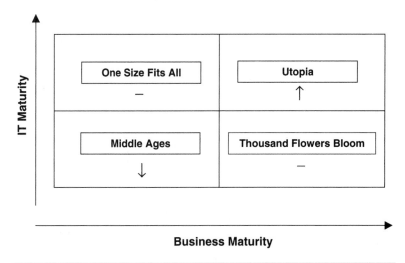

EXHIBIT 4.1 EPM Readiness Based on IT and Business Maturity

the role it can play in empowering individuals to improve performance (see Exhibit 4.1).

CURRENT STATE OF EPM TOOLS AND TECHNOLOGIES

The second barrier to EPM adoption I'd like to discuss is the current state of EPM tools and technologies. They have come a long way since the inception of EPM in the early 2000s, but challenges remain.

For example, many organizations still struggle to gain access to accurate and reliable performance information. This is a result of the situation I have already described with many organizations scattering performance information across 10 or 12 or more unconnected transactional systems and data warehouses. And despite investments of many millions of dollars in these systems, many organizations are still unable to create a single version of the truth about their performance with data integrity.

Another challenge is that business users still must rely on IT experts to gain access to management reports and analyze customers, products, revenues, expenses, and other elements necessary to make decisions about how to use scarce and valuable resources in the best way. This is because there are too many different and unconnected tools required to create and analyze reports, and most of them are tuned to the needs of report creators instead of report consumers.

Another is that deploying and managing comprehensive EPM solutions—which include transactional systems, data warehouses, and BI tools in addition to EPM applications and services—are still too difficult and expensive. This is because these solutions have evolved in a haphazard way as vendors have delivered separate products to meet the varying needs of different lines of business and functions in companies. Multiple vendors delivering unconnected products that nevertheless must work together leads to instability and higher total cost of ownership.

To address these challenges, EPM must provide an efficient and effective way for companies to achieve a single version of the truth about their performance with data integrity. In addition to enabling an accurate view of performance, data integrity provides a foundation for companies to establish performance metrics that are meaningful and consistent across the enterprise, making it easier for senior management to track progress. Data integrity and consistent metrics in turn make it possible for individuals to commit to achieving certain goals and being held accountable with confidence.

EPM must also simplify and significantly improve the experience of using performance management solutions for business users so that performing desired tasks is fast, easy, and intuitive, and does not require assistance from IT. Ease of use encourages greater participation in performance management activities across the enterprise and transforms performance management solutions into everyday business tools.

And EPM suppliers must integrate their products so that solutions are simpler to deploy and manage, less expensive, and more reliable. Lower total cost of ownership makes it possible for companies to more widely adopt enterprisewide performance management solutions.

With the problems of data integrity, ease of use, and lower total cost of ownership solved, organizations would be able to turn their attention to the activities that are the heart of performance management.

To better understand the state of EPM tools and technologies today, it's valuable to look at how they have evolved.

As previously discussed, prior to the introduction of EPM, BI was the primary tool for performance management. Over the past 20 years, BI has become invaluable for accessing, analyzing, and sharing performance information, and more recently has become even more important as part of an EPM solution.

However, because lines of business and functions in organizations have historically had different information needs, access requirements, and report preferences, BI vendors have delivered different tools to satisfy them: one set of tools for production reporting, another for ad-hoc query and analysis, another for multidimensional analysis, and yet another for data mining and statistical analysis. Even today, most BI vendors offer a set of point products, and few are tying them together as part of an integrated solution.

As EPM takes over as the primary performance management solution—with BI as an essential element—integration becomes even more important.

The need for EPM solutions to work better together extends beyond any single supplier's products. Organizations implementing EPM initiatives want to simplify their performance management solutions—applications and services, BI tools, transactional systems, data warehouses, and so on—to get fewer moving parts. The goal is to lower total cost of ownership. At the same time, they recognize that they will continue to live in a multivendor world and are looking for help in pulling it all together.

Evolving EPM to become the mission-critical glue in multivendor enterprisewide performance management initiatives is hard work—a combination of inspiration and execution—and involves solving tough problems the industry has been working on for years.

Joe Corn, a social and cultural historian at Stanford University, uses the automobile as a model for how technology must evolve to ensure adoption. In my view, his analogy is apt given the current state of EPM. Here is a paraphrasing of what he says:

Driving the first cars required skill in lubricating various moving parts, sending oil manually to the transmission, adjusting spark plugs, setting the choke, opening the throttle, wielding the crank and knowing what to do when the car broke down.

A driver today simply turns the ignition key, puts his foot on the accelerator, brakes, and steers. The complexity of modern cars—which are in fact sophisticated computers—is shielded from the driver, abstracted away and hidden by a greatly simplified and standardized user interface.

The evolution of the automobile suggests a guiding principle for future EPM development: Make it simple, but make it better.

The principle of "make it simple, but make it better" has led to the emergence of a critical next step in EPM: an EPM system. An EPM system consists of business and financial applications; a BI platform; common services such as data and application integration and master data management; and a role-based environment that simplifies access, communication, and collaboration—all integrated into a single, unified system that can be easily and cost-effectively deployed, managed, and maintained.

Part Two

───────────── ❧ ─────────────

PREPARING FOR BATTLE

~ 5 ~

Draw an Accountability Map

The key to extracting tangible and sustainable value from EPM going forward lies in focusing on five key activities: drawing an accountability map of your organization, achieving Information Democracy, building an EPM Center of Excellence, standardizing and consolidating EPM tools, and deploying an EPM system. Over the next five chapters, I will focus on each of these activities in detail. First up is drawing an accountability map.

Most executives and managers agree that defining the flow of information in their organizations and eliminating bottlenecks is a vital corporate discipline that can improve decision-making, efficiency, and performance by ensuring a common understanding of goals and accountability. Many, however, admit to falling short of that goal—and that's not surprising. It is one of the most complex tasks in modern management.

It's complex because in many organizations today, the distance from the executive suite to the front lines can be layers deep and thousands of miles long. Goals defined by top management can quickly become blurred, diluted, or even lost on their way, leaving tactical managers entirely in the dark. A sales organization, for example, may continue to focus on increasing penetration into existing accounts long after corporate strategy has shifted to expanding the customer base. The strategy may be excellent, but may fail because it has not been effectively communicated.

The challenge is compounded when the separate strands of information come from weakly linked, uncoordinated reporting systems, rendering it incompatible or even contradictory. Passed from system to system or hand to hand, information that might have been initially accurate can become distorted. Even if it is accurate, the ability to drill down for detail might not exist. And regardless of its accuracy, information that is delayed in processing or generated on an arbitrary schedule can be out of date and, as a result, useless or even misleading.

It is also clear that there is a critical need for information sharing among functional areas. Coordination of sales and marketing, for example, can make both operations more effective. Accurate sales forecasts allow manufacturing to plan production and finance to allocate resources. Information from manufacturing has an obvious impact on purchasing and human resources, and it's equally clear that poor synchronization of activities wastes resources and opportunity.

When organizations fail to define the flow of information, it is not for lack of awareness. More than ever, organizations today know they need to think and act enterprisewide. And yet, operations remain fragmented. Here's why.

Organizations and living organisms have much in common. Each interacts with its environment, draws sustenance from its surroundings, pursues goals, grows, and changes. Each competes with other entities for success and survival. And each is made up of mutually dependent parts that must function in perfect accord to survive.

The processes by which the parts of a living organism communicate and collaborate—turning stimulus into response or thought into action—are inborn. They are mapped in DNA and passed from generation to generation.

An organization, on the other hand, has no inherited mechanisms. Communication among its parts must be deliberately designed and implemented. Ironically, considering how critical communication is to a modern organization, it often takes a back seat to the daily tasks of building a business, meeting customer needs, and dealing with competitive threats. And once established, mechanisms for communication are often allowed to fall behind as the organization grows and changes.

One reason for this is that functional areas within organizations still use different information-sharing tools and technologies. These tools are purchased based on parochial needs and preferences, and do not include mechanisms for directly linking tactical implementation with the strategy they supposedly serve. The task of linking them falls to an already overworked IT department, which means that, often, information-sharing is handled manually or left undone. And the organization pays the price.

In an ideal world, information-sharing tools and technologies would enable information sharing and collaboration. Many organizations are, in fact, moving to standardize and consolidate their information sharing and performance-management tools. But most organizations are still a long way from that and must seek other solutions to the problem.

What is needed is a practical way to link strategy with a thorough overview of an organization and its interdependent functions. If that can be done, it is relatively simple to find technical and organizational solutions that effectively address strategic goals.

A technique I recommend is to engage in a process that lets top management create a top-to-bottom map of the entire organization with the goal of identifying all the places where specific functions at specific organizational levels intersect. Once the intersections have been identified, top management can add key insights about the intersections—such as the degree to which they drive the business—and relate them upstream to corporate strategy and downstream to tactical execution.

Once this discovery process is complete, it becomes possible to identify the links that must be created to ensure that information goes where it is needed within the organization, and that it flows unhindered from strategy creators to tactical implementers in key areas of the business. I call the output of this exercise an "accountability map," because it makes clear who needs to know what information in an organization and who needs to be held accountable for acting on it (see Exhibit 5.1).

The purpose of an accountability map is not to solve problems, but rather to thoroughly and comprehensively identify the areas in which solutions are required. And it is precisely this critical identification step that is missing when organizations take a piecemeal, tactical approach to selecting information sharing and performance management solutions. Once a map has been created, it becomes much easier to find technical—and organizational—solutions that effectively address strategy goals.

USING AN ACCOUNTABILITY MAP AS A CONSENSUS-BUILDING TOOL

To illustrate how an accountability map works, consider the case of a multibillion supplier of a commodity agricultural product that created an accountability map for its business like the one I just described. The purpose was to gain input from top management on what to measure and how to improve the company's performance as part of a comprehensive EPM initiative. The mapping process was also used as a strategic consensus building tool, to facilitate interaction and communication through the building of a common business language, support the

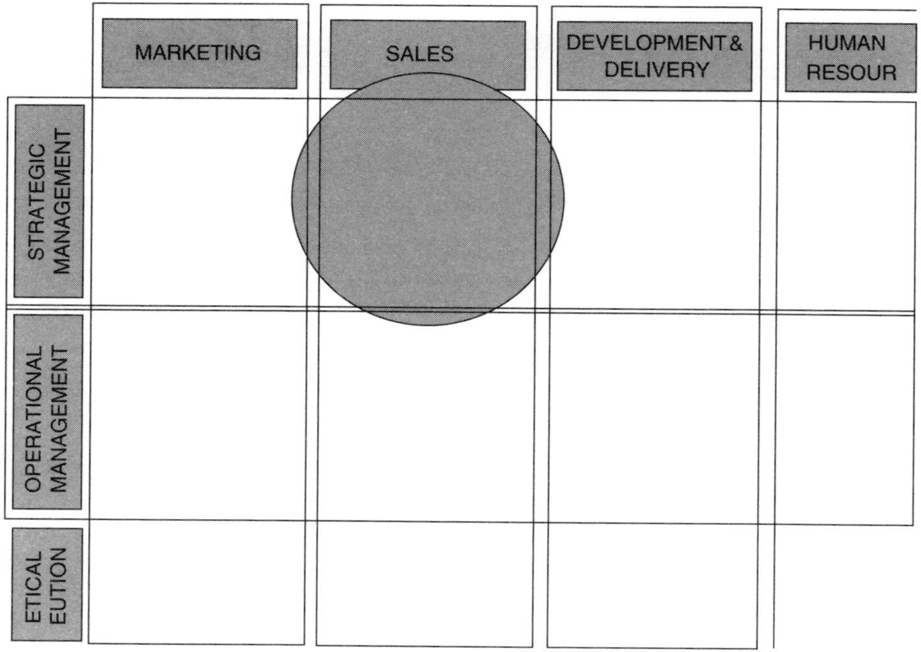

	MARKETING	SALES	DEVELOPMENT & DELIVERY	HUMAN RESOUR
STRATEGIC MANAGEMENT				
OPERATIONAL MANAGEMENT				
ETICAL EUTION				

EXHIBIT 5.1 Intersections on an Accountability Map

alignment of strategic objectives, and deliver a roadmap for EPM.

Aided by a consultant, over the course of 30 days, the company conducted meetings with key executives in each of its functional areas and top management. The mapping process covered management practices and realities in all phases of the management cycle—vision and strategy, goals and objectives, execution and evaluation. For purposes of this example, I'll focus on the company's goal and objective setting activities and processes. Going through the mapping process revealed the following:

The primary goal at the company is to maximize margin, and the mapping meetings confirmed that every group clearly understood this. However, executives also realize that setting a margin goal is difficult since the company's primary product is a commodity whose price is dictated by the marketplace.

Consequently, the company focused on the parts of the business that management can control. These included:

- Growth and diversification
- Distribution and logistics
- Operational improvements
- Portfolio scrutiny
- Risk profile

Within these areas, management would set goals based on reducing production, distribution, and operations costs and minimizing risk. Communicating these priorities within the company was not an issue, as most of the groups know how these goals relate to maximizing margin.

However, the mapping process showed that two critical elements were missing that would enable the company to more effectively set attainable goals for the organization. The first was the absence of effective ways to measure whether the goals have been achieved. The second was lack of a process for giving responsibility to the functional areas that can control or contribute to achieving these goals.

In addition, the mapping process showed that the company's decision makers were mired in too much disconnected information with no way to easily identify and eliminate activities that don't add value, no easy way to measure and track strategic KPIs, and no effective method to communicate goals and objectives.

The company understood that strategy implementation is the most important factor shaping management and corporate valuations. And the company did a great job defining strategy. The problem was that the strategy stopped at the doors to the executive suite. The company did a poor job of assigning responsibility for executing the strategy and providing effective ways to measure and monitor progress. And of course, if no one is responsible, no one is accountable.

Here are some of the specific challenges in executing strategy identified by key executives in interviews during the mapping process:

- Lack of accountability
- No method of communicating the strategy to all levels in the organization
- No clear link between strategy, planning, and forecasting
- No process for updating the strategy on a regular basis
- Difficulty in making decisions—tracking too many measures that are not strategic (mostly financial)
- Strategy and objectives are too abstract for most people
- Company does not communicate strategy to the masses simply and clearly
- No alignment of employee behavior with strategic objectives

- No way to measure strategic performance at different levels in the company
- No way to systemize existing scorecard processes and provide data more frequently

The mapping process showed that the company is challenged by the lack of a comprehensive organizational measurement system designed to affect the behavior of the managers and employees. As a starting point for solving this problem, the company had to determine which small number out of the hundreds of financial and nonfinancial measures it could track would have the most powerful effect on long-term economic performance and who should be held accountable for them (see Exhibit 5.2).

The mapping process further showed that the company needed to identify and assign accountability to KPIs across all businesses and define the ones most critical to the success of the company's overall strategy. The agreed-upon measures could then be used to provide top-level managers with a fast but comprehensive view of the business.

The process zeroed in on the key metrics—among hundreds of possibilities identified—that could be used to drive the business:

- Margin
  - By product
  - By customer (previously unavailable)
  - By location (previously unavailable)
- Margin risk
- Variable margin and variable cost
- Headcount
- Daily cash and weekly cash forecast
- Raw materials storage
- Raw materials prices

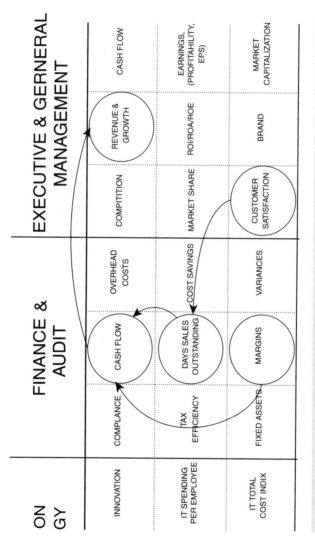

EXHIBIT 5.2 Examples of Areas Where Strategy and Execution Intersect

• Daily shipments

• Stock price

At the close of the process, the consultant recommended that the company use an interactive performance dashboard and a Balanced Scorecard-certified scorecarding application to address these issues. With these tools, the company could gain a clear understanding of corporate strategy, objectives, and accountability while proactively monitoring its actions and performance against company targets and industry benchmarks. This would help the company bridge the gap between strategy and execution, engage a broader range of employees in planning activities, and respond more proactively to changing business conditions—from each enterprise desktop to the CEO.

The company found that the process of creating an accountability map paid enormous dividends. First, it allowed top management to articulate some of the organization's biggest issues with a minimum investment of time and none of the cost or delay of other possible methods such as traditional process reengineering.

Second, it provided a clear implementation map for those who were designing a management system to meet strategic goals—eliminating risky guesswork and reducing the likelihood of extensive rework after implementation.

Best of all, building an accountability map required no leap of faith on the part of the participants. Unlike many performance management initiatives, which cannot be judged until they succeed or fail, an accountability map makes immediate, intuitive sense. It is one of those rare tools that can be evaluated in minutes but pays dividends for years to come.

⁓ 6 ⁓

Achieve Information Democracy

Information Democracy is an admirable goal, and something, it would seem, almost everyone would aspire to. But that is not the case. If it were simply a matter of applying technology to achieve Information Democracy, I have no doubt that many organizations would be enjoying its benefits today. But technology—as is always true with important changes in management philosophy and practice—is just one component of making Information Democracy work.

One problem lies in misconceptions about what Information Democracy really means. As I previously defined it, Information Democracy is a principle of equality that demands actionable insight for all. What may not be obvious from this definition is that Information Democracy is intended first and foremost to promote the good of the organization. It does this by empowering individuals, and in this way it is similar to political democracy. But there are some conceptual differences that cause the analogy to break down rather quickly.

Political democracy is intended to ensure equality for all citizens, and in so doing promote the common good of a nation. In Information Democracy, users have access to all the information and capabilities they need to do their jobs—which promotes the common good—but not equal access to all the information and capabilities present in the organization. Confusion about this distinction may cause organizations—and especially top management—to be wary of Information Democracy.

Another problem is that there will always be people in an organization who will resist change of any sort, including a shift to Information Democracy. In the words of that great philosopher, Pogo, "We've met the enemy and he is us."

Let's take a look at a few of the biggest obstacles "we" put in front of "us." The first and most common one is inertia. Even people who don't like the status quo very much believe that big change is far too difficult—perhaps even impossible—to achieve.

Another big obstacle is fear. There will always be people who fear change regardless of what it is. They're afraid that change will undermine their roles in the organization or even threaten their job security.

And finally, perhaps the most dangerous obstacle of all is self-interest. Unfortunately, there will always be people who alter the truth or mask it over for their own purposes. Similarly, there will always be people who will actively try to undermine attempts to put anything in place that threatens a power base they've built.

And within organizations, of course, "we" aren't just individuals. We also act as groups of people with common interests.

For example, IT often approaches providing access to information as a sort of narrowly focused, one-size-fits-all exercise, and although well-intentioned, this approach usually leads to enterprise reporting—not EPM.

Another camp consists of the lines of business, departments, and functions. Often they behave as if the rest of the world doesn't exist, focusing exclusively on their own parochial needs. The result is typically multiple and discrete EPM products.

Top management represents another camp. Their objective is to set strategy. To do so, they rely on many information sources, some of them reliable but many of them unreliable.

And there are the disparate work groups that share a common trait: they take advantage of the lack of a coherent strategy for EPM in their organizations, use whatever products and tools they want, and offer information and insights subjectively to whomever they want.

Despite these organizational and behavioral obstacles, Information Democracy is critical to a comprehensive performance management initiative because information stakeholders require it to do their jobs and fulfill their roles. For example:

Employees. EPM tools today are still largely implemented at the departmental level and reserved for the information elite. The good news is that more organizations are beginning to standardize a smaller set of tools available to more people. In addition, as EPM reaches beyond finance and into operational areas of an organization, it reaches more user segments: namely, workers and team leaders in charge of operational activities such as marketing, HR, and so on.

Regulators. In the wake of high-profile examples of corporate misconduct, organizations now face increasingly stringent requirements to make financial reporting more transparent. As a result, most organizations have been forced to restructure their financial reporting to comply with these regulations—an activity that typically goes much deeper than just the reports themselves. Forward-thinking organizations are taking advantage of this necessity to restructure their management reporting as well.

Suppliers and partners. As businesses offload critical functions to suppliers and others in their decentralized business networks, success depends on extending access to information across the networks. Sharing information helps businesses work with their suppliers in concert to improve the overall performance of both organizations.

Customers. Many organizations are finding increasing benefits to making information more available to customers as well. For example, car leasing companies—unable to differentiate the cars they offer—have found that sharing information with the fleet managers of their corporate clients helps them differentiate through service. And insurance companies increasingly are distributing their products and services through a powerful channel—their clients' HR departments. And, of course, Web-based businesses are finding that giving their consumer customers direct access to information about their buying or usage patterns can build loyalty.

In addition to stakeholder needs, there is another reason that Information Democracy is important. In most organizations, EPM initiatives to date have focused on cleaning up specific data sets and improving access to this data within certain departments or for a limited number of need-to-know audiences.

Information Democracy takes two critical steps beyond this: It integrates all relevant information into a single user-view, and makes this data available across the enterprise. Although not all information will be made available to every employee, Information Democracy makes the right information available to the right people at the right time.

To be sure, Information Democracy requires process and change management. This mandates a visionary executive such as a CFO becoming a Chief Performance Officer as well. And unfortunately, too often, Information Democracy becomes most feasible when there is a "changing of the guard" at the highest levels of management; for example, at the CEO level.

Nevertheless, with the proper level of executive commitment, Information Democracy can thrive and become a cornerstone of an organization's EPM strategy.

≈ 7 ≈

Build an EPM Center
of Excellence

In working to find business solutions, IT and business groups within an organization share common goals, yet their approaches are often so independent of each other that they may be working at cross-purposes. IT managers might focus on architecture, function, and standards, but lack any real understanding of what business users do. Business managers and analysts might understand the business need, but do not have the technical background to develop solutions that support it.

Finding common ground for IT and business is the concept behind an EPM Center of Excellence, which is an organization that defines, refines, documents, and promotes best practices an organization will use to deploy EPM.

WHY YOU NEED A CENTER
OF EXCELLENCE

Centers of Excellence are frequently implemented in IT environments to help organizations implement a variety of technologies, including data warehousing, BI, and the applications of assorted vendors. What these implementations have in common is the creation of a central repository of knowledge, experience, and best practices, and a big picture perspective that can assist others in an organization with similar deployments.

In a similar way, an EPM Center of Excellence can provide these and other benefits to an organization for managing business performance. It should be kept in mind, however, that some of these benefits take longer to realize than others. This is because organizations typically have a burning issue that drives their need to implement EPM, and this issue will drive the setting of the short-term goals of the Center. Over the long term, however, an organization can expect to achieve the following benefits from an EPM Center of Excellence:

Build a centralized infrastructure and expertise. Many Centers feature a lab for research, proof of concept, prototyping, and advanced training. If so, test labs, tools, and best practices can be integrated and be accessible to all project teams through one source, eliminating the need to duplicate scarce and expensive resources.

Consolidate and leverage best practices. A Center provides a vehicle that facilitates knowledge sharing. A Center also can create reusable assets and build competencies, leveraging an organization's investment in its EPM efforts.

Eliminate disparate tool usage. A Center can standardize toolsets and processes, helping to ensure consistent, cost-effective, rapid implementation of optimized processes.

Centrally administer performance management for the entire organization. This will create visibility into critical performance parameters of the delivered application, keep everyone informed, and keep applications aligned with business objectives.

Bring order and uniformity to data. This is achieved by aligning different projects that use similar data and controlling costs by reducing redundancy in data and processing.

Eliminate the problem of a fragmented data infrastructure. Fragmented data infrastructures, which are typical in larger organizations with multiple department-specific data warehouses or data marts, can prevent organizations from obtaining a complete view of customers, including management of their supply chains and monitoring business performance.

Provide a business focus. A model Center measures performance from the perspective of business and end users, creating a more customercentric organization.

Establish an enterprisewide framework deploying EPM applications. The framework can be leveraged for future development initiatives, resulting in lower costs, improved delivery times, and higher quality. It can also ensure that critical delivery components are delivered in place and help increase the quality and timeliness of information from the EPM system to near real time.

Enhance interactions with suppliers. This can be achieved by sharing the latest capabilities in EPM technology.

Control costs. By acting as a central source of EPM optimization expertise, a Center can help eliminate redundancy in EPM efforts. Often, the skills developed and the processes created by individual project teams are not shared within the IT department or across lines of business. Each team starts from scratch with each new performance optimization project—

resulting in wasted time, money, and talent. A Center can help ensure that an organization receives the maximum benefits from the resources invested in its EPM efforts.

Achieving these benefits depends on the maturity of the Center and the resources available to it. Organizations should initially focus on those objectives that promise to deliver the greatest benefit and address their areas of greatest need, and get maximum buy-in.

FIRST STEPS

Creating an EPM Center of Excellence is both practical and achievable. An organization can start small, leverage its existing resources, and expand the Center as it proves its value to the organization.

In planning a Center, it is necessary to establish a charter by defining its objectives in terms of the overall organizational objectives. A Center's objectives need to align with the objectives of the business units, the development teams, and the organization as a whole. There also needs to be alignment among executives, business users, and IT staff in their interest for EPM deployment.

A critical first step in building an EPM Center of Excellence is defining a coherent strategy for the design of EPM within an organization that will serve as guiding principles for all EPM projects.

The EPM design will then need to be broken out into logical phases, with each phase building on the previous phase and tying in to the overall EPM strategy, which is continuously evolving. As your company's EPM strategy and vision evolves over time, your Center will be your vehicle for evolving that strategy.

A Center should also define the services and deliverables it will provide. These should be based on stated objectives that will, of course, change over time as the Center matures, and as either additional resources are provided to the Center or resources are redeployed due to their more efficient utilization.

A Center should also have a plan to develop a staff capable of delivering services to its customers. This may include training existing staff, hiring new staff, and procuring outside consulting services.

The Center should define and put in place metrics to monitor its ongoing performance and progress and, in so doing, adopt its own EPM strategy around execution.

And a Center should develop a communications plan to inform the rest of the organization of the services offered by the Center and the successes it has achieved.

There are four additional necessary ingredients to creating an EPM Center of Excellence: defining the Center's roles and responsibilities establishing a reporting structure ensuring that there are human resources in the Center with the skills necessary to accomplish its objectives, and providing adequate funding.

ROLES AND RESPONSIBILITIES

An EPM Center of Excellence's main responsibilities are to:

- *Establish requirements* for EPM projects and initiatives that meet users' and the organization's needs.
- *Train users* on EPM tools, including how to access and leverage the data provided by the EPM.
- *Provide the analytical expertise* of Center staff by performing complex, ad hoc analysis for business units.

- *Ensure uniformity of analytical approaches* used to address common business issues across the organization.
- *Coordinate the definition of master data and metadata* in the organization, including the definition of common business terms.
- *Establish standards for EPM tools* used throughout the organization.
- *Develop prototypes* of EPM applications as proofs of concepts.

REPORTING STRUCTURE

There are two important considerations regarding the positioning of a Center in an organization. First, a Center must be strategically or appropriately placed in the organization in terms of level and "location." For example, a Center should be positioned high enough in the organization to be able to have an organization-level point of view and sufficient organizational clout. Conversely, it needs to be low enough within the organization to be in touch with what is actually going on in terms of day-to-day performance management.

The second issue deals with where in the reporting structure to locate a Center. Various business functions are potential candidates for housing a Center, but most commonly, a Center reports to the CFO or CIO, and in some cases, to the CEO. Occasionally, a Center reports to a corporate services executive independent of a specific functional area. Experience thus far has shown that Centers are most effective when they report to the CFO or a services group.

Wherever a Center is located, it is important that it be related to the strategic mission of the organization and is able to effectively engage in cross-functional activities. If this not the case, a place on the organization chart independent of any function may be necessary.

REQUIRED SKILLS

For a Center to successfully carry out its mandate, its staff must possess a diverse set of skills. Required abilities of a Center staff include a strong mix of business, analytical, and information technology skills. In addition, be prepared to bring in outside experts as needed; for example, consultants and vendor experts—especially for on-the-job training of Center personnel and for getting started on projects after a charter and funding have been secured but before the Center is fully staffed.

Deployment of EPM systems must necessarily be based on an understanding of an organization's business. A Center, therefore, must have a manager who has this understanding and can communicate the knowledge effectively to all constituents. Required business skills include an understanding of the needs of the various functional departments and the business issues faced by the organization, and communication skills that enable him to communicate effectively with senior managers and IT regarding EPM needs, potential, and strategy.

The ability to derive deep insight from data is also an essential capability of the Center. The use of sophisticated statistical analysis requires people with a background in operations research, or data-mining scientists. These resources are best suited to conduct in-depth analyses and build new models for less sophisticated users.

Finally, because IT will serve as the enabler that permits EPM to be deployed, a Center staff must understand how to access and manage the data needed to support the business and analysis requirements; the various IT tools and technologies, the data-warehousing and data-administration skills necessary to map EPM to business needs; and the EPM infrastructure implications of business and analytical requirements.

Ideally, a Center will have staff members with at least two of these three necessary skill sets. Potential sources for these experts include existing IT professionals who possess a strong understanding of the business, and business users who are technologically minded.

FUNDING

Various models can be used to fund a Center. It makes sense to start with CFO-sponsored funding for three to five quarters so the Center can operate at no cost to the business units. This gives the Center time to establish value and credibility. Following this period, consider a charge-back or cost-recovery method. Set the expectation well that this service is valuable and will therefore carry a cost once it is established.

By its very nature, an EPM Center of Excellence is cross-functional, and a way of allocating its cost to the various areas benefited needs to be developed. One method is to simply allocate all cost to one department. The downside is that this can lead to inefficient utilization of a Center by other departments, which use it as a "free good."

An alternative way of funding is to set up a Center as an independent profit center, with departments billed for the cost of the Center based on utilization. Care must be taken to ensure that these charges do not discourage use of the Center.

A third possibility is to have some predetermined allocation of the cost of a Center to the user departments in a fair manner. Departments will then feel free to use a Center as needed to improve their business performance. This third approach, which focuses on cost recovery, is preferred.

TASKS

Once established, a Center will perform some or all of the following specific tasks:

- EPM vision management
- EPM design ownership
- Dashboard and scorecard creation
- Report writing assistance
- Rule writing
- Data and metadata mapping
- Master data-management support
- Financial data-quality management
- Planning application development, updates, and changes, including:
  - Annual plan, operating budget
  - Revenue and expense forecast
  - Workforce planning
  - Capital expenditure planning
- Profitability analysis
- Customer churn analysis
- Cross-sell and upsell analysis
- Visualization tools
- Corporate security
- Performance tuning and optimization
- On-the-job training for advanced or "power" users
- Promoting the reuse of applications, rules, and reports

- Promoting a "common business language" including defining terms such as customer and full-time equivalent employee

SUSTAINING A CENTER

Often, organizations create an EPM Center of Excellence to address issues that have arisen from various EPM initiatives an organization has already begun to implement. This means a Center focuses immediately on addressing those issues. This also means the Center must have short-range goals and strategies to address the organization's immediate "pain," and longer-range strategic goals to address future projects.

Longer-term goals a Center may be called on to address include reducing organizational costs, providing direction for the organization's EPM efforts, or providing the organization with a central platform for performance management.

RELATING TO OTHER INITIATIVES

Another question that should be answered when building an EPM Center of Excellence is, how will it relate to other business initiatives underway in the organization, especially with regard to other IT-focused initiatives? Establishing a Center should be coordinated with the other initiatives an organization is planning both in the formative stages of a Center and on an ongoing basis.

For example, an organization may also be planning to establish a data warehouse or implement master data management. The expertise contained in a Center may help in planning these projects and ensuring they meet the organization's needs. At the same time, the Center might benefit from the expertise and planning that goes into these other projects. Either way, careful consideration and integration of an organization's initiatives are essential to ensure it leverages its IT investments and achieves the maximum possible return on its investment.

IT'S WORTH IT

Building an EPM Center of Excellence is neither fast nor inexpensive. To ensure success and ongoing support for a Center, it is important for the Center to establish its value early on. Centers that are serving the business rarely need to defend their costs.

The beauty of an EPM Center of Excellence is that it makes organizations smarter. Drawing on the team's experience and expertise for strategic deployments increases efficiency and productivity. It enables better decision making and makes the best use of the organization's resources. Ultimately, all of those benefits translate into increased performance. However, it takes commitment from a forward-thinking organization to invest in the right people and the right processes.

Sometimes, of course, this is easier said than done. In the early 2000s, a major Asian manufacturer created an EPM Center of Excellence to help drive a EPM project that was envisioned as the first of many. The goal of the first project was to bring together disparate data from many divisions into a single data warehouse.

While this initial goal was effectively achieved because of the technical competency delivered by the Center, the company's approach to building and funding the Center resulted in a high cost structure. The high cost of using the Center alienated potential users within the company, limiting the number of follow-on projects the Center was asked to undertake. And in turn, with so few projects, the Center's impact on the company's overall performance management initiative was limited.

Where the approach took a wrong turn was actually at the outset of the project, when its organization and charter were determined. The Center was planned, organized, and staffed primarily by technical experts, with little input from the company's business users. In addition, the Center reported into a central IT service group and interacted primarily with CIOs throughout the company.

Generally speaking, the Center had little contact with business managers until a project had been identified. Once a project was completed, the Center had very little contact with business users, except for providing technical support and fielding requests to make changes to applications. Because there was no strong relationship between the Center and business managers, problem resolution was difficult. In addition, to determine user satisfaction, the Center relied on an annual IT survey that covered a broad range of IT issues—not just Center issues—which meant that problems with the Center went unresolved for extended periods of time.

The situation was further complicated by the fact that the company also supported a separate vendor-specific ERP competency center, which often competed with the EPM Center for projects. This made it difficult for the company to standardize tools and a methodology for EPM projects, and worked against the Center's efforts to establish best practices.

Perhaps the biggest obstacle to the Center's success, though, was its funding model. By corporate mandate, the Center was funded by charging its costs plus a profit and fees for use of the centralized data warehouse. Together, these costs placed a tremendous financial burden on the sponsoring business units, causing complaints about how much projects cost. The Center responded to these complaints by outsourcing work to India to reduce costs with mixed results.

What this example illustrates is that it takes more than technical competency to build and sustain a successful EPM Center of Excellence. A Center must also have a suitable charter, strong support and participation from the business, and a funding model that encourages, rather than discourages, its use.

At the opposite end of the spectrum, consider the EPM Center of Excellence at Bank of America. Bank of America, based in Charlotte, North Carolina, is one of the world's largest financial institutions, serving individual consumers, small and middle market businesses, and large corporations with a full range of banking, investing, asset management, and other products and services. The company has more than 5,700 retail banking offices, more than 17,000 ATMs, and serves nearly 22 million active users through its online banking operation.

Bank of America began its EPM journey in 2003 with an initiative driven by finance to transform the company's finance organization into one that would be considered best in class in its industry. At the time, the finance organization was using legacy software and outdated hardware, and the company's financial analysts were spending 60 percent of their time gathering data needed for reporting and 40 percent of their time analyzing and reporting on it.

The company's long-term goal was to flip those percentages by rethinking the processes and automating them with advanced software and hardware systems. The benefit would be a finance organization with more time for activities that could add value to the business.

Already committed to both Lean and Six Sigma management philosophies—the former stressing waste reduction as exemplified by the Toyota Production System, and the latter focusing on quality—the bank naturally applied both to its EPM planning. One Six Sigma technique in particular—Voice of the Customer (VOC)—guides Bank of America in all its critical initiatives, including EPM. VOC is a formal process of engaging with customers to get their requirements and feedback over time to ensure better quality.

Finance thought at first that it would implement its EPM reporting and analysis project using a Big Bang approach— designing and implementing one standard approach and system for all the company's lines of business. Early VOC conversations quickly convinced finance that the requirements of the various lines of business were so different that each would have to be tackled individually.

When it became obvious that this one large-scale EPM project was more realistically a series of smaller EPM projects, the question became how to ensure an infrastructure, consistent methodology, and best practices that could be leveraged across all projects while meeting the specific needs of each line of business in each individual project? The answer was to establish an EPM Center of Excellence, which the company did in early 2004.

Unlike the Asian manufacturer previously discussed, Bank of America staffed its Center from the outset with both technology and business experts. This and its commitment to the VOC process ensured that the views of the business were constantly represented in each phase of planning, designing, and implementing each project for each line of business.

Also unlike the Asian manufacturer, whose EPM Center suffered from competition from a vendor-specific ERP competency center, once the bank's Center was established and on firm footing, it was moved outside of finance and into a shared services organization within corporate that managed a number of different competency centers. While each competency center within the bank is run by its own manager, all centers report to a single executive, ensuring that potential conflicts are more quickly and easily resolved and that centers are not working at cross-purposes.

Because the bank's Center is now staffed and run by an unbiased corporate team—as opposed to a finance team—more functional areas within the bank are using it for their own EPM initiatives. This has enabled it to fulfill its charter as an organization designed to establish standards and best practices for all the bank's EPM projects.

Also unlike the Asian manufacturer, which adopted a flawed funding model that placed a heavy financial burden on potential users that discouraged its use, the bank was more thoughtful in designing its funding model. The Center operates as profit center on the belief that it must generate funds of its own to ensure continued investment in advanced technologies, but sets pricing fairly and transparently so users always know what they are being charged and why. The Center also focuses on delivering the highest possible value while keeping costs low.

One way the Center keeps costs low is to outsource some of its work to India, just as the Asian manufacturer had done. The difference is that the bank treats its outsourcing partners as extended team members—visiting frequently, offering training, and applying the same standards of quality to them as it does to its internal employees.

Today, the bank is successfully implementing its initial automated reporting and analysis projects throughout each of its lines of business, and hosting other projects throughout the bank through its Center of Excellence. This is in sharp contrast to the Asian manufacturer, who had success with one project but struggled with subsequent projects.

~ 8 ~

Standardize and Consolidate
EPM Tools

While we often reflect on the lack of penetration of EPM solutions, it turns out that a lack of technology or tools isn't the cause. In fact, in most enterprises there are far too many tools.

For years, EPM tools have been purchased predominately on a departmental basis, by line-of-business or functional management. Sometimes, IT has been involved in the process and sometimes not. In other instances, IT has procured its own solutions, adding to the disarray. Over the years (and in most enterprises), this has led to myriad siloed implementations. Each department has its own tool with unique user paradigms, proprietary formats and metadata, different data extracts and transformations, and business semantics.

The costs associated with this sort of fragmentation are extreme. There are the direct costs, such as software licenses and maintenance. And then there are the indirect costs associated with supporting multiple products: more complex and time-consuming internal support, change control, and the training and cross training of users.

Finally, there is the less tangible—but far more critical—effect: the impact on the business, which includes operating inefficiencies, inconsistent treatment and leverage of common customers, competing internal strategies, and misalignment with corporate direction.

Part of the answer to this problem is the standardization and consolidation of EPM tools and technology.

STANDARDIZATION

Standardization in this context means choosing a tool or tools that will be used widely and consistently within an enterprise. To do this, you must first develop a set of criteria for selecting standards. These criteria must be extensive and balanced. You must consider the technology and architecture, and the nature of the company that provides the technology. For instance, is the company financially stable and growing? Is it an easy company with which to do business? Does it have a global reach? Are the company's customer references credible?

Developing these criteria will involve establishing a small team, ideally within an EPM Center of Excellence if you have one. In addition, business users must be actively involved in the process. You will want to identify and enlist power users throughout your organization to help. While the users you select might already have a strong allegiance to a particular tool and/or vendor, there is an important twofold rationale for enlisting their help. First, they are the most likely individuals to know the requirements for EPM tools. Second, they are also the most likely individuals to resist the adoption of new tools. By engaging with them early on, you stand a better chance of neutralizing that resistance.

To avoid skewing the criteria in favor of an installed tool, it is important to define some basic ground rules, for instance: "The vendor must have x customers and revenues of x dollars," or "Product functionality must extend beyond simply query and reporting to include modeling, scenario development, OLAP, and data mining."

Establishing a standard for future purchases, although complex, is far easier than consolidating a whole host of existing tools, which is the next step in the process.

CONSOLIDATION

Consolidation means reducing the numbers of redundant tools used for EPM. On average, most enterprises have between 7 and 12 redundant EPM tools.

However, this does not necessarily mean reducing the number of tools to one. Instead, the goal should be to have a set of consistent and integrated tools to support the majority of EPM application opportunities that arise.

Consolidation is difficult because users in general are reluctant to change, and specifically might be reluctant to give up a tool they are comfortable using for an unknown. Even if they are unhappy with their current tool, they may be reluctant to accept a new one. To ease the process, here are some basic steps to follow:

1. **Make a strong case for consolidation.** Business needs change rapidly, and EPM tools must keep pace. This argument alone makes a case for replacing outdated tools or tools from vendors that have failed to stay competitive. And of course it goes without saying that the best reason of all for eliminating a tool is if the vendor who offered it is out of business and no longer making updates or offering technical support.

   A tougher sell because it has less of a direct impact on users, is to make a case for achieving better return on investment or reducing costs by eliminating redundant tools. For example, a smaller set of nonoverlapping tools means that companies can more easily gain experience, establish best practices, and deploy tools more rapidly because less training is required. On the cost-savings side, having fewer tools means fewer tools for IT to support, less training, lower licensing costs, and greater leverage.

Still, no matter how good your case, expect the process of consolidation to take between 9 and 18 months, depending on the size of the user community and the number of established tools. Create a project plan, with specific milestones and responsible parties, to gauge progress.

2. **Work with business management and purchasing.** Your goal is get these groups to formally support the standard and to ensure that nonstandard tools cannot be purchased by end users.

3. **Pick the low–hanging fruit first.** Find those users and departments that are willing, and (perhaps) even eager, to embrace new tools. Do everything possible to ensure that their migration and training go smoothly. This will help to build confidence and a positive track record, which will make future projects easier.

4. **Engage some of the skeptics early on.** Once all of the willing users have been migrated to standard tools, it's time to "win over" the more skeptical and resistant users. Usually by engaging some of those skeptics early on, there will be fewer "holdouts." However, fear of the unknown and inertia are substantial obstacles. For most of those users who are reluctant to migrate, education will be the best weapon. Classroom training, tutorials, and handholding will help.

5. **Discontinue technical support.** Finally, for those who refuse to give up their old tool (there will be a few), you should strongly consider discontinuing

technical support, even though you may have to allow them to continue using the tool. Hopefully, their numbers will be small.

While the standardization of tools and technology has many benefits, standardization alone is insufficient to address the many business issues that arise from a fragmented approach to EPM. I often ask businesspeople how many definitions of "customer" they have in their enterprise. This is typically met with a knowing chuckle, as every organization has many definitions for customer (sometimes with good cause). The same is true for definitions of other entities, such as products, employees, suppliers—and business processes (for example, order processing).

As with tools, standardization of business semantics is another area in which an EPM Center of Excellence can help by taking the lead in driving toward common definitions for key entities and processes that need to be modeled, analyzed, and measured.

~ 9 ~

Deploy an EPM System

The last key to extracting tangible and sustainable value from EPM is implementing EPM tools and technologies as a unified system. Here are some points to consider when selecting an EPM system.

As previously discussed, EPM is an accepted methodology that enables organizations to improve their competitiveness and efficiency, reduce business risk, achieve strategic alignment, improve agility, and improve collaboration between individuals and business units. An EPM system supports the pervasive adoption of the EPM methodology by moving EPM toward greater value and efficiency, enhancing its capabilities while making it simpler to use and significantly lowering total cost of ownership.

For example, an EPM system should solve the lingering problems of data integrity and ease of use, making it possible for everyone in an organization to access relevant performance information and use connected performance management tools as part of a complete performance management cycle.

An EPM system should also enable out-of-the box performance management solutions for specific functional areas. Examples include workforce planning for human resources; compliance for finance; and customer profitability for sales—logical extensions of the core capabilities of

EPM in planning, financial reporting, business analytics, and management reporting.

Done right, an EPM system should include shared business information, common processes, and services. It should seamlessly integrate all of the different elements of performance management solutions so that distinctions between applications and services, BI tools, transactional systems, and other data sources are irrelevant to both business users and IT experts. It should create more interoperability between stages in the performance management cycle. And it should bring a new level of consistency and alignment to performance management activities across the organization.

In summary, an EPM system should enable organizations to:

- Make aligned decisions across an enterprise based on insights derived from one version of the truth
- Understand the impact of changes across the enterprise
- Continuously reduce the latency between the occurrence of a business event and the realignment, communication, and execution of strategy and plans
- Create transparency and visibility across the enterprise
- Connect people, processes, and other systems in an optimal manner in order to become a performance driven enterprise
- Minimize the total cost of ownership of EPM
- Scale and leverage data, users, and applications to allow for faster future growth

EPM SYSTEM COMPONENTS

Just as ERP systems transformed the way organizations conducted and tracked day-to-day business activity, an EPM system must streamline the way organizations are being directed and managed. Therefore, the best type of EPM system is one that supports the management processes business users engage in to work collaboratively on shared information, rules, and logic—regardless of the specific task they are undertaking at any point in time.

For example, before EPM systems it was not uncommon for a user to move back and forth between a budgeting application and a sales forecasting application to complete a planning update task. With an EPM system, when users move from one management task to another, it should appear that they are using the same system, with the different applications they are using abstracted and invisible to them. And it should be easy to share data between the tasks. For this to happen, an EPM system must support the following:

- Business users must have access to EPM applications that are specific to their needs and not generic management applications. They should also be able to draw on domain knowledge and best practices from subject matter experts (internal or external to the organization).

- Business users sharing an EPM application should be able to continually refine the application to meet their needs. If this is not the case, business users will revert to their spreadsheets (or worse). Organizations need to make the EPM system as "user friendly' as possible to encourage adoption of the system.

- It must be possible to link individual EPM applications into a network of applications that covers the entire organization. This network could eventually extend beyond the organization to cover customers, suppliers, and partners in an extended supply-chain model.

- It must be possible to implement EPM incrementally, driven by business users and focused on current business priorities, rather than as a monolithic enterprise application project. Otherwise, implementation becomes an inhibiting factor in meeting its own goals of agility.

To meet these other requirements, the components of an ideal EPM system are best-of-breed EPM financial and business applications, a BI platform, an EPM environment, and common services.

The following sections describe the components of an EPM system and include real-world examples of companies using these components to solve performance management issues (see Exhibit 9.1).

EPM APPLICATIONS

Financial Management

Financial management software should be a comprehensive application that delivers global collection, financial consolidation, reporting, and analysis in a single, highly scalable solution. Financial management should use today's most advanced technology, but it should be owned and maintained by the finance team, not IT.

An example of a company that utilized EPM financial management applications to speed data collection and financial consolidation is Global Hyatt, a global enterprise that operates more than 200 hotels and resorts in more than 40 countries around the world. Global Hyatt specifically uses financial management software to more quickly and efficiently consolidate its financial data and streamline planning processes in its 200+ far-flung business units.

The catalyst for change at Global Hyatt was the growing realization that a manual process of aggregating financial

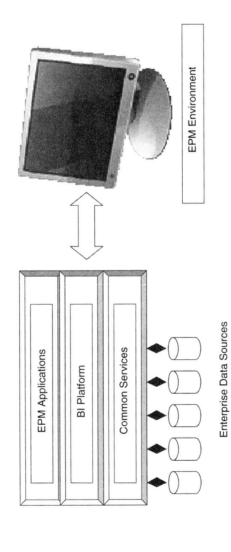

EPM Environment

EPM Applications

BI Platform

Common Services

Enterprise Data Sources

EXHIBIT 9.1 A Unified EPM System

data, which relied on spreadsheets, had become far too time consuming. The process of consolidating operating results so management could gauge hotels' operating performance on a monthly basis was taking 15 days or more, consolidating results from its legal entities into the corporate structure was taking anywhere from 45 to 75 days, and the company's budgeting process anywhere from three to five months.

In addition to the length of time needed to perform these activities, Global Hyatt had issues with the accuracy of its data because using so many different spreadsheets was both time consuming and error-prone.

Global Hyatt began its initial EPM implementation in 2004 and was operational in less than six months at every Hyatt-managed hotel in the Americas, Europe, and Asia. All hotels now use EPM financial management for financial consolidation, budgeting, and forecasting.

Since implementing the application, Global Hyatt has reduced individual property month-end closing time to two days, reduced the time it takes to complete its forecasting process, and improved data accuracy and compliance.

Beyond the time savings, Hyatt top management believes that the single most important benefit of EPM is that people within Hyatt responsible for managing performance can now track data directly to its source in a timely way. This means the right people are getting the right information at the right time.

Planning

Planning software should be a centralized, Web-based planning, budgeting, and forecasting solution that drives collaborative, integrated, event-based planning processes throughout the enterprise for a wide range of financial and operational needs. Planning should allow companies to track and monitor business plans and forecasts translating strategic objectives into operational goals and targets, and should replace outdated spreadsheet systems with multidimensional, driver-based forecasting processes.

An international mining and exploration company is an example of a company using an EPM planning application to manage its rapid growth. In just three years, the company grew from a fledging operation to a global company with three mining operations. The company owns and operates gold and copper mines and a base and precious metals operation in the Pacific Rim.

One way the company encourages growth and outstanding performance is by tying bonus compensation for its employees to specific KPIs. But because its ERP system did not have an adequate planning function—essential to setting and tracking performance goals—the company decided to implement an EPM planning application that would allow it to plan and track operational performance across the enterprise on a daily basis. This would require full visibility into KPIs almost on demand, which meant that the planning application would have to be much more than just a budgeting tool.

Having successfully implemented an EPM planning application, the company is now able to produce daily and weekly reports with one click, and obtain and communicate a real-time view of how physical statistics from its mines will affect financial performance. These statistics include measures such as tons of materials mined, processed, or trucked; equipment availability and utilization; safety statistics; and types of drillings performed.

In addition, the planning application lets the company graphically visualize a statistic—such as the amount of product it has available—and see how it is trending day by day to get a sense of performance for the month. By comparing that to forecasted stockpiles, for example, its marketing department can determine whether it will be able to meet production targets and adjust shipment and truck schedules accordingly.

Because much of the company's business operations are in remote locations, it keeps the information flowing through dashboards and automated report distribution via email on a daily basis, rather than having to wait until the end of the week or month. This allows the company to manage operational and financial performance side by side.

Another company using an EPM planning application successfully is one of the world's largest mobile communications companies. Headquartered in Europe, its decision to implement an EPM planning application was driven by a reorganization that created a need to do planning and reporting on new and previously unaligned activities. Due to different management information structures and systems within its operating subsidiaries, the company realized it needed to adopt a very different approach from the one it had been taking—an approach much more rigorous and standardized.

For example, the company was having problems with information consistency because there were no detailed structural guidelines for data collection in its subsidiaries. Data was being entered manually into a variety of different group applications, and reporting from groups to corporate was based on verbal definitions of content.

The first decision the company made was to develop a common information warehouse for management reporting, and the first step in building that was to develop a whole new conceptual management information model. A major requirement of the new system would be to harmonize both financial and operational information, and provide standardized approaches to planning and reporting. Given the disparate nature of the systems in use within the company, the new system would also have to be capable of providing a high degree of efficiency, transparency, and uniformity. And this would require a single reporting language.

Once the conceptual model had been agreed to, a planning application was chosen based on its capability to support the model, the single reporting language, and the scale and complexity of the company's information needs. With the help of a consultant, it implemented the new system.

To understand how the new system works, consider the company's requirements to understand and track two critical KPIs—subscriber segment profitability and sales channel profitability. This data is sourced from local operating company finance systems and allocation drivers from operational warehouses. And even though the number of data items is large—around 100,000—the company now has a common view of these profitability KPIs and can drill down into them to create new views of profitability based on new organizational responsibilities.

In fact, the company can drill down into all of its KPIs—around 700 of them with 24 dimensions—in more detail than it could before. For example, because the company can now split revenues into six dimensions, it can see how much revenue is generated by consumer customers through its own shops in a given country, based on type of payment and service used.

This deeper level of analysis requires large amounts of data behind the system—nearly 50 times the data in the previous system. One of the key benefits of the system is that it integrates data sources and different forms of information delivery, which makes managing and using this large amount of data easier.

Modeling

Modeling software should let executives and managers understand the full financial impact of alternative strategies. Instead of spending time on building, maintaining, and training finance employees to use cumbersome spreadsheet modeling tools, modeling software should deliver pre-packaged modeling and forecasting so finance experts can better spend their time testing alternative strategies, building contingency plans, and understanding the impact of those strategies and plans on an organization's long-term performance.

A UK-based company improved its strategic commercial and financial decision-making capability through the use of EPM modeling. Based in London with operations around the world, the company is an engineering and construction contractor for the oil and gas industry that designs and delivers complex projects in harsh and challenging environments.

Several years ago, the company found itself in a weak financial position having suffered significant losses on several major turnkey projects. When a new management team was brought on board to effect a turnaround, among its first actions was to stabilize the business by selling off noncore assets and raising equity finance to strengthen the balance sheet.

With these survival steps behind it, top management initiated a strategic review to develop a clear strategy for growth, which involved a complete review of the business based on a bottom–up financial model. Previously, the company had used a spreadsheet-based solution for financial modeling and planning. However, the solution was not integrated with the balance sheet and provided no means of generating information about shareholder value add. It was clear that management needed a modern, more integrated tool for its strategic review.

The company chose a modeling tool that was flexible and had a high level of data integrity built in, so the company could produce financial models with integrity to minimize risk and create efficiencies. Because time was of the essence, it hired a consultant to help with the development and implementation of the application.

One of the first actions the company took when the modeling solution was up and running was to run through it a growth strategy that had been developed prior to the acquisition of the tool. The exercise showed that the strategy—which had been modeled using the old spreadsheet-based tool—was not likely to deliver the levels of top-line revenue growth or bottom-line margins the company was expecting from it. This resulted in significant and necessary debate among top management about how to refocus and refine the company's proposed strategy.

The new modeling software also was critical in translating the new strategy to highly accurate and detailed models that showed potential outcomes. These models gave top management the confidence it needed to move forward with the new strategy.

EPM modeling software did more than eliminate the company's reliance on spreadsheets for basic financial modeling. It also allowed it to more efficiently perform more sophisticated analyses such as cash flow projections, capital structure alternatives, rating agency and bank reporting; covenant and ratio analyses, and liquidity analyses with confidence. These capabilities gave the company far greater insight into its financial decisions before they were made.

Dashboards and Scorecards

Dashboards provide views into various key operational and financial metrics, while scorecards help align corporate strategies with individual goals so each performer is helping the organization achieve its strategic objectives.

Preformatted reports have been the traditional face of EPM to business users in the enterprise, but they are rapidly being replaced by dashboards. Dashboards are rising in importance because front-line staff, managers, and executives don't need more static data. Instead, they need true insights that help them make decisions, react to exceptions, and help ensure accountability. The most effective dashboards apply appropriate analytics to source data and present the resulting information in a way that makes actionable events or trends immediately apparent to the user.

Dashboards also play an important role in combining financial information with operational information to provide a more complete view of performance. This more comprehensive view is crucial because financial metrics alone do not tell the whole performance story.

Dashboards are not a new tool in the enterprise, but it's safe to say they've undergone an extreme makeover in recent years. Dashboards of the past were created solely for executive management to provide a visual snapshot of business activity. In contrast, today's dashboards are often extended to all business users, regardless of rank. As such, dashboards play an important role in moving enterprises closer to Information Democracy.

Another difference between the dashboards of yesterday and those of today is that dashboards used too little interoperability and few linkages to root cause, while root cause is a cornerstone of today's dashboards.

While it may be easy to distinguish between dashboards of the past and the present, some confusion remains concerning the differences among dashboards, portals, and scorecards. All can play important roles in EPM in the enterprise—especially when used as parts of a complementary strategy—but the differences matter.

Portals bring structured and unstructured information together into a common architecture, and in so doing can simplify access to multiple systems. However, portals generally do not have intelligent linkages between systems and therefore cannot integrate information, business processes, or workflows. While they can be complementary to dashboards by providing an interface for delivery to a broad audience, their limitations relegate them to a relatively minor role in performance management.

In the context of EPM, the more relevant distinction is between dashboards and scorecards. Scorecards enable the tracking of personal measures, scores, and actions by a person, team, or division in the context of how they relate to overall corporate strategies. Scorecards play a major role in aligning overall corporate strategies with individual goals by providing each performer or performance unit a clear picture of how they are helping the organization achieve its strategic objectives.

Dashboards perform a different function. Dashboards leverage enterprise data resources to present business users with clear, actionable information about current and historical performance in the context of planned or expected performance. They give users all the information they need—including financial and operational information—in a highly graphical, intuitive format. And they make it easy for users to investigate and explore further, if necessary, to ensure a smart, timely business decision.

In fact, "timely" is a key descriptor of dashboards. Take the example of a bank that is running a geographically dispersed global network of ATMs. Each machine in the network has variable status information that is time sensitive, including how much cash it has, whether it is working, and whether there are any timed outages. Either on demand or via alerts, banks should have answers to these types of question within minutes—not in weekly or even daily reports.

Simply put, scorecards answer the questions: How does my goal support the corporate strategy? How am I doing? Dashboards answer the questions: How did I miss my goal? What should I do to get back on track?

By enabling critical business decisions, dashboards offer some of the best returns on investment (ROI) among performance management solutions today. They allow managers to intervene quickly when things go awry. They highlight immediate and long-term opportunities. They are powerful tools for cost control. All in all, dashboards deliver tremendous business value—especially in light of the fact that they leverage many of the IT investments an enterprise has already made.

Dashboards also offer dramatic productivity gains for business users, although most enterprises will go through an initial discovery process to evaluate and understand the impact dashboards will have on their users. In addition, dashboards provide a means for keeping users informed and aligned so that everyone in departments and business units everywhere in the enterprise is on the same page. And, dashboards improve communication between different departments and functions across the enterprise, empowering users to collaborate in solving problems (see Exhibit 9.2).

With the value of dashboards as a performance management tool firmly established, interest has shifted from "why" build dashboards to "how to" build effective dashboards more quickly and easily. To address this need, development efforts should focus primarily on more effective ways to identify which KPIs should be tracked using dashboards, and how to empower users to create their own customized dashboards and refine them over time, without burdening IT.

Creating and deploying KPIs throughout an enterprise can be a time-consuming and expensive process. Companies need dashboards that centralize and simplify this process so that nontechnical business users can quickly get the information they need and spend more time on higher value activities.

Business users are looking for drillable decision flows that can quickly guide them from summary metrics to diagnostic metrics to root causes so they can make decisions in near real time using up-to-the minute information. Further, these dashboards should tap into all data sources in the

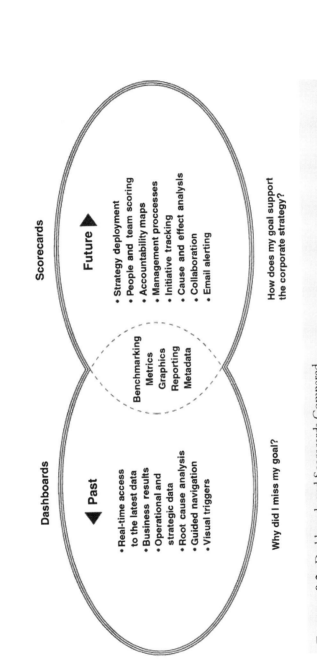

Dashboards

▼ Past

- Real-time access to the latest data
- Business results
- Operational and strategic data
- Root cause analysis
- Guided navigation
- Visual triggers

Why did I miss my goal?

Scorecards

Future ▲

- Strategy deployment
- People and team scoring
- Accountability maps
- Management processes
- Initiative tracking
- Cause and effect analysis
- Collaboration
- Email alerting

How does my goal support the corporate strategy?

Benchmarking
Metrics
Graphics
Reporting
Metadata

EXHIBIT 9.2 Dashboards and Scorecards Compared

enterprise to provide a consistent and comprehensive view of KPIs everywhere in the organization.

Top management should be able to communicate strategy, set targets, establish accountability, and monitor KPIs using recognized scorecarding methodologies and industry benchmarks. Lines of business managers should be able to personalize and monitor their own KPIs in one place, making performance information meaningful and easy to understand. Financial controllers should be able to quickly see variances in spending while sales managers are tracking deals as they close. And call center supervisors should be empowered to explore why call times are increasing.

In short, because individuals in different lines of business and functions have different needs, the ideal dashboard software will provide a codefree, wizard-driven process for all these dashboard creators so they can quickly design personalized dashboards and deliver them in a secure manner—even when users are traveling.

A large U.S transportation company decided that dashboards were the best way to achieve its goal of finding a tool that would let top management take the pulse of a functional group's performance in the moment. For that purpose, the company's tool of choice was a dashboard created as an interface to its existing BI system.

The performance management challenge the company wanted to address was to provide its IT leadership team with a tool that would provide at-a-glance insight and drill-down capabilities into the key indicators of the organization's health as it related to strategic initiatives. Key indicators for the group included growth, service levels, efficiency, people, and ease of doing business. The desire was to gain insight that would enable management to identify problems early to avoid or minimize negative financial, operational, or customer impact. In addition, management wanted to store historical data to be leveraged as metrics for continuous improvement.

The overriding goal, however, was to link IT performance to business results. The company had a business strategy determined by executive management and the company
wanted to demonstrate specifically how IT was supporting
it to show alignment.

The project team determined early on that it wanted
to build a dashboard that would display timely information
at a summarized level and would include status indicators
to reveal the health of any defined attribute. The team also
established as a requirement capabilities that would allow
users to drill down to uncover additional detail.

To deal with the first challenge, the project team established a real-time data warehousing approach based on
existing data warehouse technology that would feed a snapshot of current and past IT operational performance to the
dashboard. By displaying data pulled from multiple sources
in a coherent and meaningful format, the dashboard would
serve as a window into the group's performance. Making
this happen involved shifting from traditional mainframe
batch processing to real-time file processing from UNIX;
gathering data from different platforms; and allowing authorized users to update data to simplify the process and
reduce maintenance.

The second challenge was met by using the company's
existing BI tools to build a single application that could pull
data from multiple sources to produce a single version of
the truth.

Before going live with the application, the project team
did an enormous amount of user acceptance testing. They
held weekly meetings with users to demonstrate progress
and to ensure the application was meeting user expectations. They appointed a primary user in each individual
subject area to test and have final approval of the parts of
the application dealing with that subject. And they created
an IT dashboard mailbox to allow people to communicate
any bugs or deficiencies during testing.

Another example of a successful use of dashboards is an initiative undertaken at one of the world's largest seafood companies designed to give the firm at-a-glance performance snapshots of individual functional groups.

Every company has a supply chain, but for this company that supply chain begins when the company collects and fertilizes eggs in a hatchery and ends when it sells fish to a supermarket. As a result, the company has a wide range of reporting needs. For example, its agriculture division is interested in fish growth rates, while its processing staff needs operational data.

In addition, some of its operations are in remote locations and have limited telecommunications capabilities. Therefore, the company needed a way to make sure all functional groups got the information they needed without relying on high-speed communications.

The company had implemented an ERP system and a basic reporting application in 2002 and was running its reporting processes using a series of intricate spreadsheets. To update information, employees would have to rekey data and email these spreadsheets around the company.

It didn't take long for the company to realize that this reporting solution was inadequate. In particular, it needed a solution that would allow users to log on and find their own information so the company would not have to provide centralized management and support.

To meet these requirements, the company implemented an analytics and reporting application and created a Web portal to store reports and to give users access to them. Users could run or refresh about 160 different reports, and a small group of power users could develop their own reports and do sophisticated analysis, drilling down to raw transactional data if they wanted to.

But the real breakthrough from a user point of view—especially for nonexpert users—came when the company decided to automate KPI information and display it via dashboards. This allowed the company to develop some KPIs that would have impossible to report on manually. For example, one of the company's most important KPIs shows the company how much it earns for every kilo of raw materials. It is the KPI against which everything is measured and too complicated to track and report on using spreadsheets.

In addition, dashboards gave nonexpert decision makers access to performance information that enabled them to continually guide the direction of the company. For example, having up-to-date sales information enabled sales and marketing staffs to more effectively plan promotions and create and update budgets. And accessing dashboards turned out to be a good way for employees in remote locations to easily access performance information.

As a next step, the company will automate the creation of dashboards and deliver simplified report views for a greater proportion of its workforce.

To further illustrate the distinction between dashboards and scorecarding, consider the travel company for which scorecarding was a better choice than dashboards for meeting its objective, which was to foster collaborative strategic planning in its corporate travel accounts. This scorecarding application delivers a single vision while meeting several operational business objectives, including service level measurement, account management, and operations. The solution allows the company to communicate and discuss common goals and objectives, making it clear to employees where they should be concentrating their efforts to help their company and travel programs meet strategic business objectives.

This company's scorecarding solution arms managers and executives with drill-down access to accurate, integrated data so they can measure performance against key corporate objectives including cost containment, customer satisfaction, and high-quality customer support. Because the solution inherently encourages bidirectional communication, employees can actively align their specific activities with the overall corporate objectives. In addition, individual scorecards cascaded from corporate business objectives ensure that each employee can track and measure his or her results against those corporate objectives.

Because performance scorecards are available on each desktop via the Web, employees are now able to view real-time financial, customer, and reservation data previously unavailable to them. This has enabled the company to transform the traditional role of travel counselor from order taker to business partner by supplying front-line managers with analytical tools they need to gain real-time data that assists them in their daily decision making. This has made it possible for the company to change its customers' view of the firm from simply a service delivery vendor to strategic partner.

One of the largest pharmaceutical companies in the world is another example of a company that uses scorecarding to improve performance, in its case, to drive common, consistent, and optimized processes throughout the company. A primary strategy of the company is growth through acquisition.

One outgrowth of building the company through acquisition was that operational services and enabling functions were deployed in very different ways throughout the company. This was particularly true within the company's Research & Development division, where operations were managed in distinct silos with very different business models, internal processes, decision-making processes, and even IT systems.

In a pharmaceutical company, R&D is the engine that drives future growth, as it is responsible for discovering and developing new and innovative medicines. Consequently, the operational areas within R&D were a logical first area of focus for the firm's EPM initiative.

The company's primary goal was to optimize the productivity of researchers by integrating processes, systems, and governance models, minimize operational distractions, and drive a common way of doing things globally, while maintaining the right degree of site individuality.

Another goal was to establish a culture of continuous improvement rather than a flavor-of-the-month initiative, so the long-term sustainability of the effort was of paramount importance.

The solution consisted of three distinct elements working together: a new strategic framework designed to ensure global alignment with the company's objectives; a new matrix operating model that encouraged and facilitated cross-site collaboration and knowledge sharing; and a comprehensive initiative that leveraged a scorecarding application and the Balanced Scorecard performance achievement framework developed by Kaplan and Norton, and other techniques such as Six Sigma to drive continuous improvement.

A new strategic framework had to come first because historically, every year during the business planning process, various teams would establish a new set of strategic objectives for the year. But they would fail to cascade throughout the organization in a timely way. Kaplan and Norton stress making strategy everyone's day job, but the company had been previously unable to achieve this state. By the time people began to understand and act on the company's strategy, it had changed.

To remedy this, the firm made the decision to lock down its vision and high-level strategy for a three- to five-year period and let a more dynamic annual goal-setting process accommodate changing business conditions.

With a new strategic framework in place, the firm's R&D division next developed a new operating model for cross-site collaboration and knowledge sharing. The new model shifted from a geographic operating model to a matrix operating model in which cross-functional teams meet for the sole purpose of driving best practices and optimized processes.

The initiative's scorecards support the new strategic framework and operating model, measuring performance and identifying improvement opportunities by comparing performance across sites or, in some cases, against external benchmarks.

Scorecards allow the company to measure performance over time, but also enable its divisions and groups to align with overall corporate objectives. Scorecards initially were created using a top-down design—allowing certain executives to drill down within functions or sites—but they now are bidirectional, giving functional or site managers the ability to drill up to determine how the performance of an individual unit affects the overall performance of a division.

Implementing the three-pronged approach first in its R&D operations enabled the company to test the concept and gain enough confidence to begin a more comprehensive rollout to other units within the company. The initial R&D implementation also gave it the chance to prove its tangible benefits. Within the first year, using scorecards to increase the visibility of improvement opportunities in its R&D operations had already netted the company $12 million in process improvements.

Reporting and Analysis

Collecting data from disparate systems, operations, and geographic locations in order to accurately report to internal and external audiences remains one of the greatest challenges financial managers face today. Financial reporting applications should satisfy the broadest range of financial reporting needs and generate formatted, book-quality financial and management reports that comply with regulations and external requirements. This helps control and increase operational efficiencies.

A large European telecommunications company was able to literally reinvent its finance function with EPM reporting and analysis software. Driven by the pressures of privatization, this company changed in many ways—culturally, operationally, and financially. Deregulation led to decentralization. Autonomous business units were formed as a way to speed up decision-making and to take advantage of market opportunities in the go-go 1990s. However, everything changed in 2000 when the company went public just as the dot-com bubble burst and the telecommunications market plummeted.

In 2001, the market slowdown drove the comapny to introduce a companywide cost-cutting program. At the same time, top management was naturally seeking more information to help them make strategic decisions that would improve company performance. As a result, one of the six strategic areas of the company targeted for performance improvement was the finance organization. By improving the efficiency and quality of information coming from the accounting departments, the company had the opportunity to raise the level of performance across the company.

Over the years, decentralization had led to a proliferation of ERP and reporting systems. Each company within the parent company had its own accounting staff and chart of accounts. In one country alone, the company used almost all the ERP systems being marketed there. The processes within various accounting departments were minimally standardized, so consolidation and reporting across the company were cumbersome due to process diversity and the lack of a common data model. All this made it time consuming and costly to roll up finances.

As part of its renovation, finance identified five major initiatives. One was to consolidate its 36 accounting organizations into one separate legal entity operating in three locations. This shared service now makes it possible for the company to standardize and streamline its accounting processes and minimize duplication of effort.

In tandem with the creation of this shared service, the company standardized on one chart of accounts to make shared accounting services efficient. Without a common chart of accounts, accounting staffs must apply different rules and definitions for different business units. That makes it more difficult to combine divisional financial information into a companywide financial report and get all decision makers to agree on a single version of the truth.

A third project is aimed at process automation and standardization. Finance is on a mission to find ways to use automation and best practices to drive costs down even further. In fact, the shared service is a perfect example of how, following the upheaval of combining 36 groups into one, the company can more easily refine and automate the processes employed there to increase efficiency and improve quality and accuracy. And the company finds it easier to achieve return on investment in technology and process re-engineering when the investment occurs only one time in one location and in an operation of larger scale.

One example is the cumbersome process of resolving internal trades, in which goods and services traded among business units are tracked so that they are not double-counted as part of corporate revenues or costs. Since the process automation initiative, all business units process internal trades using the same rules and procedures.

The last two finance projects are related to information systems. The company has standardized on one common ERP system, down from the seven systems it had previously. The company is also implementing a single EPM system to align critical corporate functions, such as planning and reporting, tie strategic plans with business unit execution, and ensure companywide focus on key value drivers, such as customer satisfaction and technical innovation.

Due to the company's fragmented structure, it was crucial to have the support of top management in establishing a shared services model for accounting across business units and legal entities.

Key to the successful implementation of the shared service, the company introduced a market-based pricing model—as opposed to cost-based pricing. Prices vary based on factors such as quantity of invoices processed and whether they are paper-based, scanned, or electronic copies. This pricing model helps business unit CFOs better understand what drives their accounting costs. It also makes their costs more predictable and creates incentives for them to increase their efficiency even further by using automated services that are more favorably priced.

In addition, service level agreements were established for each of the company's five main business units to regulate the relationship between the business units and the shared service. Key performance indicators were introduced to measure performance at both the shared service unit and the business units. The company felt it was necessary to formalize all these aspects of what is essentially an in-house relationship because it minimized the problems inherent in a fragmented company with strong business units.

The business case for common accounting and ERP systems was not as compelling for some of the company's smaller business units, and this presented a challenge for the project team. However, with a clear mandate from top management and a strong business case that these efforts would benefit the company as a whole, the smaller units were convinced to cooperate. In a standardization initiative such as this, it is crucial for all groups to participate.

Driven initially by cost concerns, finance went shopping for software applications that would help it streamline its business management processes, such as planning, budgeting, analytics, scorecarding, and reporting. The company expected to simply choose the best of breed and the most cost-effective tool in each category. It soon became clear how strategically important it was to have all these fit together into an integrated whole to drive performance improvements. In addition, limiting the number of graphical user interfaces people need to adopt is important in making the most of a new analytical platform.

The company uses an integrated business management model that starts with strategy: establishing goals, value drivers, plans, budgets, performance agreements, and incentives. It moves through the implementation stages to what it calls "follow up," which includes analyzing results, issuing reports, and using a balanced scorecard to monitor the value drivers and see if business areas and overall corporate strategic objectives are met.

By having all these functions work tightly together, reporting can be used, for example, to identify and explain significant deviations from plans, and help determine corrective action.

The company's integrated architecture supports better fact-based decision making by balancing and organizing value drivers across enterprise functions. It looks at five major categories of value drivers: customer/market/society measures, employee skill and learning, internal processes, innovation, and financial measures.

One reason that the integrated approach is changing the corporate culture is that it changes what people at the company base their decisions on. Integrating the management cycle and focusing on value drivers helps quantify and institutionalize intangibles or "soft" measures, such as brand position or customer satisfaction.

In fact, the company's customer focus has been strengthened as part of its integrated management process as it continually and systematically elevates customer feedback to higher levels of management, thereby building better knowledge and competence.

Another example of how this new approach improves how the company manages itself is in the business review process. Traditionally, business reviews of critical issues were conducted using scorecards, and results were manually compiled in PowerPoint. Many backup slides would be produced, in case a specific question was raised, many of which were never used. The company has now standardized its business review processes, which will lead to greater collaboration across functions in defining value drivers, designing report structures, and preparing and analyzing business reviews. In addition, it has automated this process with a scorecarding application, which eliminates the wasted effort spent on slides that are never needed.

At the end of the day, however, a successful performance management system depends on good data to drive analysis and insight. At this company, linking high-level summary data with the underlying detail helps managers understand what drives results in their groups.

A common data model unifies the company's new finance systems. This streamlines the deployment of the IT systems and makes it easier to identify further opportunities for cost-saving process standardization because detailed and comparable analysis enterprisewide is available at the touch of a button.

In addition, a common data model helps finance put reports together quickly and reduces the chance that executives will misinterpret what the reports tell them.

A common data model also makes it possible to link high-level reports with the detailed information that feeds into them. This helps decision makers better understand the dynamics that led to the results. In today's post-Enron era, having an explicit link between high-level and detailed information increases transparency and improves the audit trail.

Common data also prevents managers in different groups from basing decisions on different—possibly conflicting—information.

And finally, simplifying the information structure at a company dramatically lowers the cost and time required for implementing and maintaining IT systems.

At this company, common data populates an EPM system that performs budgeting, analysis, reporting, and performance scorecarding, making the entire performance management cycle more streamlined.

Planning reports that used to take two days to produce now take half an hour, and two-thirds of the finance staff's time was taken up with transaction processing. This has been dramatically reduced, so finance now spends more time analyzing the information instead of just compiling it.

By leveraging the analytic capabilities resident in the finance function, the company is locally tapping an efficient and centralized source of performance improvement and decision information, which has important organizational repercussions. In fact, the finance function has become a driver for change, and that is something new.

Another example of a company that uses EPM reporting and analysis software to satisfy its needs for both internal and external planning is Logitech, the global provider of personal interface products for the digital world. Although in the case of Logitech, performance came first.

Logitech is a fast-growing business in which double-digit top-line growth has often been the norm, not the exception. The company's bottom-line growth can be even faster.

Fueling the Logitech engine is accelerating worldwide demand for Logitech's array of products—computer mice and keyboards, webcams, headsets and speakers, gaming peripherals, iPod/MP3 accessories, and remote controls. Logitech ships hundreds of millions of products in a single year—one every few seconds.

Staying on top of such a fast-moving, global business is a challenge that puts continual pressure on Logitech's internal business systems and processes, but one that Logitech has addressed through a combination of a progressive approach to financial management and EPM. At Logitech, finance is viewed as a business partner to its operating counterparts. The company has also invested in systems that largely automate the fundamentals of financial management, freeing up time in finance to add business value.

Logitech was already an information-driven company when it first decided to explore EPM in 1999. Logitech's IT group had successfully implemented a comprehensive ERP system and a sophisticated data warehouse. And Logitech's employees around the world were diligent about keeping the information in the company's data warehouse up to date.

But the company's finance department was still preparing management reports manually using spreadsheets. In fact, Logitech was suffering from a common malady. Having invested so much in powerful transactional systems and a data warehouse, the company was spending considerable time and effort making sure the systems worked well and data was current. But the company hadn't taken the next step necessary to unlock the valuable information trapped in those systems. It was all there, but mostly unavailable to operating executives and decision makers who could use it to monitor performance and make better decisions.

To tackle the problem, Logitech looked first at the company's flagship management report, the 3B report, which tracked billings, bookings, and backlog. Members of the finance team would prepare the 3B report manually, using spreadsheets, and publish it every Monday morning. The 3B report was a static weekly summary of orders, shipments, and margins by region, channel, and product as compared to plan, and was read avidly by the company's top executives.

Not only was once a week too infrequent, another attribute of the 3B report that frustrated executives and finance alike was that it was static, which meant that as soon as it was published, the finance team was flooded with requests for format changes and additional detail.

Despite its shortcomings, the 3B report was an important and highly visible management report in the company—the perfect place to start a far-ranging performance management initiative.

In October 2001, Logitech deployed an advanced analytics and reporting platform and began to develop a billings, bookings, and backlog application that would include dashboards specific to each set of users. The application was designed to automatically extract relevant information from the company's data warehouse on a nightly basis and organize it into standard reports that would be posted on Logitech's intranet and available to each user from his or her desktop throughout the day. The tailored dashboards would facilitate easy viewing and analysis of complex data.

Just two months later, Logitech produced its first automated 3B report. Posted every night at midnight, the report was current, presenting detailed information about sales by customer, region, product, and channel over various time periods, and the company's standard margin for that day. It was also dynamic. Using tools accessed via dashboards, executives could perform advanced queries and analytics to see data not presented in the standardized report.

The new and improved 3B report became so popular in the company that many executives replaced their newspapers with the 3B report as the first thing they read in the morning.

One obvious benefit of having automated the 3B report was that Logitech's finance team was no longer consumed with producing it manually. In addition, the 3B report improved data integrity throughout the company. With executives being able to access current information on demand, finance no longer had the luxury of correcting errors before publishing a final report. Instead, the company put greater emphasis on ensuring that the data in its data warehouse was correct going in.

Equally important, the new way of preparing and delivering the 3B report changed the mentality of the management team at Logitech. Instead of waiting to be told what their numbers were, executives were actively coming to finance with questions about variances they were seeing themselves.

On the strength of the 3B report, supplemented by other reports, Logitech began holding biweekly refresh meetings. In this meeting, every executive would present an up-to-the minute analysis of what was happening in his or her area. This increased coordination on companywide goals and made it easier for each business unit and person to be held accountable for individual goals.

With the 3B management report as a foundation, Logitech then turned its attention to its financial consolidation and reporting processes, implementing an EPM financial management application. At the time, it was taking Logitech more than three weeks to close its books. With Sarbanes-Oxley looming on the horizon, it was imperative that Logitech close faster.

After implementing the new application, Logitech regions were closing within one week and the company was able to complete its global consolidation a few days after that. The entire process could be done routinely in two weeks.

BI PLATFORM

BI platforms are a collection of tools and technologies organizations use to develop applications that enable them to access, analyze, and report business and financial information. They should ideally include tools for query and reporting, OLAP (online analytical processing), data mining, and advanced analytics, and end-user tools for ad hoc query and analysis and enterprise-class query, analysis, and reporting. In addition, BI platforms should include dashboards and scorecards for performance monitoring and production reporting against all enterprise data sources.

The importance of advanced analytics in a BI platform cannot be underestimated. However, many people misunderstand and misuse the term "analytics," equating it with plain reporting. Analytics is distinct from reporting in that it involves the aggregation, calculation, allocation, and extrapolation of data. And analytics is playing an increasingly important role in performance management in organizations today because business users work in an agile world. Today's insight is tomorrow's old news. Organizational structures have become more fluid, making the company's organizational chart look like a dancing octopus, and business hierarchies change on a daily basis.

On the face of it, ad hoc query tools might appear to be a good solution to this issue of rapid change in business. Ad hoc query tools offer business users the flexibility of making every single combination of information possible. But they don't tell business users anything about which combinations of information are the right ones to be looking at. And different people performing ad hoc queries to get at data to solve the same problem will likely end up with different answers because they have the flexibility to go about it in their own way. Good management practices argue for collaborative teams in problem solving, yet collaboration grinds to a halt when collaborators arrive at their different answers to the same question using the exact same data.

Viewed this way, ad hoc queries may do as much to institutionalize poor results and poor practices as using spreadsheets.

There's nothing wrong with ad hoc query technology, but it needs controls in the form of standard, static reports checked, double-checked, and checked again. The problem is that static reports may enable efficient data delivery, but they don't meet the organization's need for flexibility.

What organizations need instead is a system that lets business users roam freely, exploring information and analysis, yet secure in the knowledge that the data is always right. End-user empowerment is a beautiful thing, as long as everyone is using the same set of lenses to view the data and has a set of guardrails that prevents them from straying off the path. And that's where analytics comes in. Analytics allows users to freely move through large sets of data, allowing them to compare data, and drill down into lower levels of detail. The predefined model within analytic engines ensures that the outcome is guaranteed and certified correct. Users have flexibility and IT can ensure quality—impossible with ad hoc query tools or spreadsheets.

Among the most important advanced analytics requirements of a BI platform are:

Multisource, scalable reports. The ability to provide highly formatted, highly analytical reports against multiple operational data sources—with high throughput and scalable to thousands of reports and users.

Adaptive visualization. Capabilities that make this enriched analytical insight easier to consume by automatically providing the most appropriate visualization for a given data set.

Guided analytics. Capabilities that make the accumulated best practices and patterns of analysis used by expert users available to every user by automatically suggesting model relationships and navigation flows that would not be obvious to the novice user.

For instance, the expert user might know that the bad debt expense field becomes relevant to a user when the accounts receivable field exceeds a certain threshold. When such a relationship is modeled, the novice user is automatically guided along an analytic path that leads the user from accounts receivable to bad debt analytics when such a threshold is passed.

The key benefits of such an approach to advanced analytics are:

- The BI platform can address the data needs of users, and support the BI process end to end by enabling production of rich and compelling content.
- Businesses can rapidly understand the impact of operational decisions on their financial bottom line within a single BI environment.
- Businesses gain management reporting that brings together both external and internal reporting needs.

Given this view of the importance of advanced analytics, a BI platform should have, at a minimum, the following:

- Complete management, financial, and operating reporting
- Self-service report creation
- Rich interactive performance dashboards and scorecards
- Advanced analytics including advanced visualization and guided analysis
- A rich set of programming tools that enable developers to rapidly develop and deploy new applications

In addition, the BI platform should be based on open standards, certified against existing ERP systems, use the same security and administration, leverage the same metadata, and share the same look and feel.

EPM ENVIRONMENT

To provide simplified access to integrated tools and activities, an EPM system must have a unified user environment—a single, intuitive, easy point of entry to all the capabilities of the EPM system. An EPM environment should be *the* place where users conduct all their performance management activity. It should link all tools and applications, enable quick and easy access to all relevant reports and information, and provide advanced dashboards and visualization techniques.

A unified EPM user environment should also present all relevant information by groups and users in a single user paradigm. All objects should be accessed, stored, and interacted upon using a single set of actions. Content within objects can then be combined to form new objects, and users can easily move from one activity to another while retaining the context of the previous one. Sharing and collaboration can also be conducted within this environment by simply selecting objects and adding properties to them or dragging them to the intended workflow.

And an EPM environment should provide capabilities executives and managers need to better manage—not just run—the business. These include:

- Creating dynamic models and plans based on a single version of the truth with data integrity and supported by analysis, with revisions easily captured and reported across the enterprise
- Cascading goals and strategies across the enterprise and linking operating plans and metrics to each other at every level
- Providing everyone in the enterprise with a view of performance that links individual goals to corporate goals with key metrics highlighting successes and problems as they occur

To function effectively, an EPM environment must be supported by a technology foundation enabling the integration that makes the entire system easier to deploy and manage, and lowers total cost of ownership.

COMMON SERVICES

The final component of an EPM system is a collection of common services that provide all the shared services, data integration, and data access required in an EPM system. These should include:

- User services
- Data services
- Collaboration services
- Workflow services
- Abstraction services
- Calculation services

Ideally, the common services should be based on a Service Oriented Architecture (SOA), which despite all the hype and confusion surrounding it is simply a set of software design principles that have existed since the early 1990s. SOA principles state that software components should be designed as independent services with clear interface boundaries that do not rely on the state of other services. Using SOA makes EPM more Web-friendly and more deployable, hence the buzz. The bottom-line benefit of SOA is lower total cost of ownership.

Other capabilities an EPM system's common services should provide include:

- Common user provisioning—one place IT can control all of an enterprise's EPM users without having to jump around from product to product

- A unified repository so all performance information is in one place
- Centralized licensing (management), which is good for customers worried about compliance
- Support for other enterprise software systems
- Support for master data management (MDM), which helps ensure consistency of all master data across all enterprise systems such as ERP and other transactional systems and EPM applications. This eliminates costly manual processes. MDM is so central to delivering a successful EPM solution that any solution without it is incomplete.

THE POWER OF MASTER DATA MANAGEMENT

In meetings with enterprises seeking better ways to manage performance, it rarely takes me more than five minutes to identify the people in the room responsible for managing master data. They are the ones who look the most harried and harassed. Managing master data is one of the most difficult, time-consuming, and expensive challenges facing IT professionals in enterprises today, and there are few good solutions to the problem.

Master data management is not a new problem. Enterprises have been struggling with it for some time. However, new global regulations and the increased interest in EPM have given it a new urgency: compliance and performance management both require consistent master data across an enterprise.

For those unfamiliar with the term, "master data," also known as "reference" data, is data that is shared across systems and used to classify transactional data. For example: John (Sales Representative) who works in California

(Territory) sells 10,000 (Quantity) of a new widget (Product) to a customer (Customer) based in New York (Geography) for $50,000 (Total Sale) on December 15, 2005 (Date). Taken together, this information is about one transaction, but included in the transaction are individual elements of master data—Sales Representative, Territory, Quantity, Product, Customer, Geography, Total Sale, and Date. These individual elements must be identified and changes to them managed across the enterprise to ensure data integrity. Without data integrity, transaction data cannot be analyzed or reported in a meaningful way.

But that's not all. Individual elements represent master data, and the way elements consolidate or aggregate for reporting represent master data. Even for something as simple as geography, there might be multiple ways an enterprise would need to consolidate to meet all of its internal and external reporting needs.

In addition, there are typically attributes and properties associated with individual elements and aggregations, and these represent master data. One financial institution I know of has more than 700 attributes per cost center.

It's easy to see the importance of master data. Master data drives the execution of both enterprise back office systems such as ERP and EPM solutions.

It's also easy to see why managing master data is difficult. There is a lot of master data, and changes to master data are driven by changes in the business—and for most enterprises, change is a constant. Even in my simple example, changes to master data would need to occur with the introduction of a new product, the addition of a new sales rep, or new product pricing. These are everyday events in most enterprises. I know of a bank that makes at least 10,000 master data changes every month.

To complicate the situation even further, many enterprises maintain master data separately in multiple source systems. Imagine the enormity of the master data management task in an enterprise with thousands of changes across a dozen or more systems every month.

With a problem of such importance and magnitude, one would think that enterprises would have long ago adopted an elegant solution to master data management. Not so. Master data management is one more of those expensive manual processes that cry out for an automated solution.

How do most enterprises manage master data today? Remarkably, for something so important, they do it through hallway conversations, telephone calls, and email. For example, if a departmental manager wants to add another cost center or management wants to move facilities from human resources to finance, the business decision must first be approved by all the relevant decision makers. This takes time.

Once the change is approved, IT gets the request to make the change and ensure that it ripples through all the enterprise's transactional systems, data warehouses, and EPM solutions. Because changes are made manually, often the result is a lot of people making a lot of mistakes with a lot of mission-critical data—mistakes that go undiscovered because of a lack of visibility or traceability in the process.

Clearly, master data management is a problem for both business users and IT professionals in the enterprise, and there must be a better way. The ideal solution, in fact, is to manage master data across multiple systems from a centralized point and automatically rather than from within specific systems and manually.

To some enterprises, their existing ERP systems seem like a good candidate for driving such a solution. But individual ERP systems cannot provide a unified view of all the data in the enterprise, and cannot link all the transactional and performance management solutions at work in the typical enterprise—many of which today have been implemented at the departmental level and are not linked across the enterprise.

The ideal MDM solution is one that automatically synchronizes master data across all the systems in the enterprise—not just across some solutions—and is part of an EPM system.

To understand the power of such a solution, think back to the departmental manager who wanted to add a new cost center. Instead of starting a long process with a manual request, the manager would get on an EPM system and make the change himself. The system would then automatically use a formal, rule-driven process to make sure all approvals for the change are obtained and that the change is propagated throughout all enterprise systems.

An example of a company that credits an MDM solution with allowing it to more aggressively pursue acquisitions is a Fortune 500 company that has been delivering financial products and services to its customers for nearly 150 years.

As any company that has acquired another company knows, acquisitions can wreak havoc on data consistency. For example, when this institution acquired a bank in 2001 that was approximately one third its size, it caused a massive explosion of data points in the general ledger. At one point, the company had more than 2.5 million data points and 30 to 40 financial accounts being added each month. With no one group responsible for the oversight of master data hierarchies and consistency across all systems, monthly changes to master data hierarchy had to be done manually—a costly and time-consuming process.

In addition, the interdependencies and implications for individual systems were vast, considering the data environment. On the general ledger alone, there were more than 11,000 cost centers and 2,500 accounts that represented more than 1 million open relationships and more than 100 companies.

Recognizing the seriousness of the master data management problem, the bank's top management created a new group to manage it. The group developed a rigorous workflow-based process of submission and review, which included a formal board of review with representatives from the regulatory, tax, general accounting, finance, and financial systems groups to eliminate duplicate, immaterial, or inappropriate cost centers and accounts and to ensure the approved ones were in the correct hierarchies. This resulted in a 75-percent reduction in account additions.

Still, the actual ongoing process of managing change across all financial master data hierarchies—including cost centers, entities, companies and their respective relationships, attributes, and properties—was daunting. To handle these changes, the bank implemented an MDM solution that automatically synchronizes master data across all the systems in use in the bank.

With these improvements in data quality and consistency, the bank can pursue its aggressive growth strategies—including acquisitions—with confidence.

THE FUTURE OF EPM SYSTEMS

From the perspective of today's business users, there is growing demand for an EPM system that will address all their performance management requirements. Adding to the challenge, most organizations cannot afford to replace their existing infrastructure, so an EPM system must work in conjunction with as many existing systems as possible.

From the perspective of IT, which is tasked with serving its customers while ensuring reliability and scalability, any technology they deploys must be built on modern IT architecture standards. As previously mentioned, SOA is the architecture of choice because it enables all the components in a complex IT infrastructure to interoperate quite easily and efficiently, and significantly reduces the time and effort for systems to be integrated.

Beyond this requirement, IT organizations also are looking to maximize value from a smaller set of trusted vendor partners, thereby lowering their total cost of ownership. This value is magnified by addressing existing pains associated with deploying multiple, disparate, reporting and analysis tools, and various packaged analytical applications. As these have proliferated throughout the enterprise with varied degrees of planning and centralized control, IT has been left to manage multiple vendors, installation processes, hardware, operating systems, and user interfaces. An EPM system must address all these issues in a significant way.

For business users, as EPM systems evolve, they must deliver on the following requirements:

An EPM system must provide the right information at the right time in the right format to the people who need it. A modern management system must provide people who manage performance in organizations with access to timely, accurate, and meaningful information—not just raw data—they can trust. To be available in a timely way, information must reside as close to business users as possible. To be accurate, it must be based on consistent master data. And to be meaningful, it must be made available to them in reports and formats that are relevant to their roles in the organization.

In addition, people must have direct access to a set of tools for advanced analysis, reporting, and collaboration.

And both information and tools must be "always on"—available to them on the Web, on the go, in the office, on the desktop—with the system actively delivering the information and alerts they need.

An EPM system must support and link management processes, enabling people to connect past results and present plans into scenarios for the

future that predict outcomes and results. Just like the management activities it supports, an EPM system must be flexible and fluid, able to accommodate processes that are constantly changing.

Consider the example of planning. In organizations today, most planning processes are disconnected, and what's needed to connect them are a shared assumption base and a common language so the organization achieves greater forecasting accuracy, a tighter understanding of past performance, and the ability to predict future outcomes.

And, ideally, the processes that support planning would be assembled by the people actually involved in the planning process—the business users and not IT.

For business users to effectively assemble processes, they need workflow technologies and an analytical engine, process controls built into the system, alerting tools, and a process design engine.

An EPM system must support decision management. An EPM system should be able to record the decision-making process, making it easier to audit how and why business decisions are made so best practices can be captured and embedded into future behavior.

An EPM system must facilitate collaboration and information sharing. Collaboration and information sharing are essential to better decisions. Therefore, an EPM system must allow individuals within an organization to communicate, share insights, and document the discussions that are part of the decision-making process for knowledge management purposes—ideally as an anytime, anywhere, any device activity.

~ 10 ~

Comprehensive View of Performance Management

With a clear understanding of how to overcome the barriers to EPM adoption, we now can pull everything together into a comprehensive view of performance management. The view starts with the Nine Tenets of the Performance-Accountable Organization, first mentioned in Chapter 3, and how they map to the four core activities of a continuous performance management cycle, discussed previously. Armed with that knowledge, we can move to the specific business problems that can be solved by applying the core processes of the management cycle. And finally, we can link specific elements of an EPM solution to specific business problems.

TENET #1: FINDS TRUTH IN NUMBERS

A single version of the truth guides performance at all levels of the organization.

Business Challenges

Fragmented financial and operational information is siloed in transactional systems or locked away in spreadsheets.

Impact

- Managers have poor insight into enterprisewide performance drivers.
- Organizations find it impossible to access relevant information in a timely way.
- Managers find it difficult to create comprehensive and consistent management reports.
- Decisions made on partial information are unreliable decisions.

Solution

Deploy an integrating BI platform to gather data from multiple transactional systems and transform it into one insightful version of the truth about an organization's financial and operational performance that is timely, accurate, relevant, consistent, and controlled. Use dashboards to deliver information in formats that make sense and promote good decisions.

Outcomes

- Organizations close the gap between management needs and the limitations of transactional systems.
- All managers have the same facts and metrics with which to identify KPIs.

- All managers have a common understanding of what drives overall business performance.
- Decisions are fact-based and reliable.

TENET #2: SETS ACCURATE EXPECTATIONS

Every part of the business is directed by a shared commitment to strategic goals.

Business Challenges

Business goals and strategies are confined to management suites and the boardroom and are not translated into meaningful performance metrics managers can be held accountable for.

Impact

- Wasted resources as different parts of the organization pull in different directions.
- Managers optimize for the success of individual business units.
- Situations worsen when strategic plans are refined to reflect changing business conditions.

Solution

Use scorecarding and dashboarding applications to communicate realistic and obtainable goals (as established in planning), and establish performance metrics and accountability. Broadcast goals to drive strategic focus throughout the organization. Continually review and confirm for managers that their local goals are in strategic alignment with corporate objectives.

Outcomes

- Managers see the big picture and understand how their activities impact the strategic plan.
- Organizations plan dynamically without fear of creating strategic misalignment.

TENET #3: ANTICIPATES RESULTS

A thorough understanding of business drivers and KPIs leads to an ability to anticipate results.

Business Challenges

Goals are set using financial metrics only. Existing business systems are not designed to support new management techniques based on value and balanced indicators, which require broader categories of metrics, new processes, and the ability to integrate transactional data with contextual data. Tools typically enable managers to evaluate potential improvements only at the local level within their own business units.

Impact

- Historic financial metrics are the only form of performance feedback.
- Organizations are locked in to outmoded techniques for planning and measuring performance.

- Performance improvements are isolated within business units and may favor one business unit at the expense of another.

Solution

Provide managers with strategic financial and business modeling applications that support valued-based management techniques such as EVA, Balanced Scorecard, Six Sigma, the virtual close, and rolling forecasts. Combine contextual information such as industry benchmarks, customer satisfaction surveys, and call center reports with concrete financial metrics such as revenue, profits, and cash flow. Encourage collaborative modeling of potential scenarios through the use of shared business models to achieve a detailed understanding of factors that drive future performance.

Outcomes

- Managers reduce risk by anticipating business outcomes before decisions are made.
- Managers innovate by finding ways to leverage opportunities to the benefit of the entire organization.
- Organizations measure performance against metrics that matter, closing the gap between stakeholder expectations and actual performance.

TENET #4: PLANS WITH IMPACT

Insight and dynamic processes produce actionable plans that continually guide the organization to success in changing conditions.

Business Challenges

Static annual plans developed by individual business units working alone are locked in spreadsheets.

Impact

- Plans may not factor in cross-functional interdependencies.
- Managers may optimize their business units, knowingly or unknowingly, at the expense of other business units.
- Plans cannot be adapted to changing conditions and quickly become obsolete.
- Organizations are unable to react quickly to changing conditions and become uncompetitive.

Solution

Adopt a practice of continuous planning and deploy planning, budgeting, and forecasting applications that support collaboration among all managers at all levels across the organization. Explicitly represent the relationships between different business units and their interactions within a dynamic planning process that links goal setting and strategy to models, plans, and execution, and aligns individual and corporate goals. This includes the operating plan and rolling forecasts, and capital expenditure planning, workforce planning, marketing planning, and so on. In other words, enterprise planning.

Outcomes

- Managers collaborate in centrally managed planning by modeling scenarios for the future, setting new directions or making midcourse corrections, and communicating changes throughout the organization quickly and easily.

• Planning is an agile business process.

TENET #5: ACHIEVES ON-DEMAND VISIBILITY

A system that combines data from existing transactional systems across the enterprise gives managers transparent access to performance information anytime, anywhere.

Business Challenges

Current tools for performance monitoring require managers to proactively locate information from multiple sources and compile it themselves.

Impact

• Organizations are unable to drive strategies into operational plans.
• Organizations find it difficult to evaluate performance against plans.
• Organizations find it impossible to accurately anticipate results in a continuous and timely fashion.

Solution

Provide all managers at all levels throughout the organization with defined dashboards and scorecards with automatic flags, enabling on-demand access to relevant, actionable information.

Outcomes

- Managers review budgets and income statements, track KPIs, and flag variances and potential problem areas through alerts and triggers.
- Managers perform more detailed comparisons and analyses of specific aspects of performance against internal and external benchmarks through custom inquiries.
- Managers make informed decisions and take action more quickly.

TENET #6: DELIVERS CONTINUOUS PERFORMANCE IMPROVEMENT

A commitment to knowledge and understanding produces insight that drives continuous performance improvement.

Business Challenges

Actual business results often do not match planned results. The most common tools for understanding these variances are BI tools. BI tools provide managers with information—historic, simple analysis, and statistical predictions—that enables them to understand how their business is performing at any moment in time. However, they lack support for management processes.

Impact

- Managers are left on their own to act on information.
- Continuous performance improvement across the organization is impossible.

Solution

Provide managers with analytical tools that enable them to perform detailed analyses to determine the causes of variances between actual and planned results. The tools should offer a holistic view of information from strategy to operational details, and link into applications that help managers report and act on what they learn.

Outcomes

- Insight to manage and improve financial and operational performance is continually generated and distributed throughout the organization.
- Managers are supported with management processes and business systems as they make midcourse corrections or improvements to ensure reliable results.

TENET #7: REPORTS WITH CONFIDENCE

Detailed, integrated, and accessible financial and operational information enables executives to personally certify business results.

Business Challenges

Today's consolidation and reporting processes and tools are often based on inconsistent metrics and lack a single reporting infrastructure.

Impact

- Consolidating financials takes too long.

- Organizations find it impossible to demonstrate performance of key variables that significantly impact performance.
- Managers cannot create comprehensive management-oriented reports for internal use and reports for external use that comply with statutory reporting requirements.
- CEOs and CFOs are reluctant to personally certify their organization's financial results, as required by Sarbanes-Oxley.

Solution

Deploy a single financial management application that enables global financial consolidation, reporting, and analysis. Embrace the concept of a "virtual close." Document and catalogue all forms of management information (structured and unstructured) in a standard way at the level of granularity that reveals true performance drivers, enabling end-to-end reporting.

Outcomes

- Organizations deliver timely, accurate, consistent, and comprehensive financial and operational reporting.
- Organizations trim days or weeks from their close cycles.
- Information about KPIs is transparent.
- Organizations can report openly and comprehensively on business performance with confidence.

TENET #8: EXECUTE WITH CONVICTION

Truth, clarity, and confidence forge a powerful link between strategy, plans, and execution.

Business Challenges

Planning processes and tools lack mechanisms for clearly communicating required actions, progress to date, mid-course corrections, and the best courses for future actions to all managers, at all levels, across the enterprise.

Impact

- The link between planning and execution is broken.
- Managers make unreliable decisions or optimize for the performance of their individual business units.

Solution

Create a closed loop system by synchronizing the planning process with information gathering and analysis, performance monitoring, and communication mechanisms.

Outcomes

- All managers understand required actions.
- Potential challenges and performance issues are highlighted and communicated at or near real time.
- Midcourse corrections are made immediately and monitored on demand.
- Managers produce reliable results.

TENET #9: STANDS UP TO SCRUTINY

A comprehensive approach to performance management meets the highest standards of accountability and confidence.

Business Challenges

Organizations struggle with performance accountability because of poor insight into performance drivers, static planning practices, ineffective performance monitoring, and limited reporting capabilities.

Impact

- The organization's drive for performance accountability is undermined at every turn.

Solution

Building a performance-accountable organization—and even more important, sustaining it over time—requires a commitment to insight, management processes, and business systems that let managers link strategy to action, plan dynamically, monitor performance on demand, and ensure compliance. This is the work of EPM, which enables organizations to translate strategies into plans, monitor execution, and provide insight to manage and improve financial and operational performance.

Outcome

- Organizations can understand, model, plan, and manage business success.

A CULTURE OF ACCOUNTABILITY

One additional element remains in creating a performance-accountable organization, and that involves creating a culture that supports one. This is not a trivial undertaking and requires at least as much planning and effort as determining requirements and selecting an approach, tools, and technologies.

As discussed in the opening chapter, Thomas Malone believes that a democracy-like increase in participation is an inevitable outgrowth of decentralization. In a decentralized business, for example, employees need more autonomy. They aren't always close to headquarters or even to their managers, and therefore need to be able to make decisions and solve problems without being told what to do. With this new freedom comes more knowledge, expertise, and opinions—which means they'll have more say in how their organizations are being run.

Malone didn't use these words, but to be successful in this new world, organizations and the people who lead, manage, and work in them must create a culture of accountability.

A culture of accountability exists when everyone in an organization takes responsibility for his or her own decisions, actions, and their outcomes. For examples, people who work in organizations that have a culture of accountability often do the following:

- Step out from behind their job titles to act on behalf of a customer or the company
- Take responsibility for results rather than blame others for their own lack of performance
- Proactively initiate projects, ideas for improvement, and working relationships
- Face problems and challenges rather than hope they will go away

People who embrace accountability do these things because they are in the best interests of the business and—as employees and participants in the success or failure of the business—themselves.

They also do these things because they have the freedom to—freedom that has been granted to them in an organization that knows you can't ask for accountability if you do not provide Information Democracy.

And they do them because they know they are ultimately responsible for the success (or failure) of their business. If they don't do these things, who else will?

Studies show that people are more likely to embrace accountability when they have a personal financial stake in the outcomes—for example, when they hold meaningful equity stakes, own stock in the company, or when their compensation is tied to performance.

But what's interesting is that studies also show that accountability is as much a state of mind as it is a state of being. This is because for many people, money is a motivator but not the primary motivator at work. For many—and in truth for all of us a good bit of the time—our state of mind influences our on-the-job behavior far more than the state of reality.

However—and make no mistake about this—a culture of accountability is not for every organization or everyone. Some organizations—and especially the leaders of some organizations—are very content with a centralized, rigidly hierarchical organizational structure and a command-and-control management style. These organizations would find creating a culture of accountability far too threatening to their authority.

And some people are quite fearful of the accountability. Some people prefer fixed job descriptions, little or no influence over the important decisions affecting their organizations, and little or no control over their jobs. Some people prefer just putting in their time and going home at the end of the day. These people, of course, would not thrive in a culture of accountability.

But assuming you want to, how do you create a culture of accountability?

It starts with leadership at the top. To build a culture of accountability, top leaders must believe that people really are critical business assets and not just costs to be minimized.

And leaders must embrace new ways to empower people to achieve excellence without fear of unleashing the power of people.

This is an important and necessary foundation. But there is more. Building a culture of accountability also depends on each person understanding his or her personal and team responsibilities.

Let's start with the personal and consider the following questions: Are you a role model for taking responsibility, or do you pass the buck to the next person? Do you see yourself as a coach or a white knight self-appointed to save your direct reports? Do you give your staff the authority to make decisions and act independently of you, or do your own needs for control create dependency?

How you perform as a team member is equally important. For example, how respectful are you of the different roles played by each member of your team and the different skills each brings to the team? How open are you in sharing information that could help other members of your team and the team as a whole perform better? How willing are you to have your own progress—or lack of it—made visible to other team members, not to be humiliated but as a way to enlist their help in solving problems?

Finally, success also depends on the entire organization adopting some basic practices that encourage people to take personal responsibility. While there are many things you could do, in my view, there are seven things you *must* do:

1. **Communicate your goals and strategies clear to everyone.** Give people the information they need to understand where the organization is going and what role they play in getting it there.

2. **Make it clear that everyone contributes.** Set realistic goals, communicate expectations, and hold everyone accountable.

3. **Make it personal.** Connect the success of the company to that of each individual.

4. **Equip your people.** Give them the education, training, and tools they need to perform.

5. **Have confidence in others.** Give decision-making to the "experts," the people who are closest to the front lines of the business and give them permission to act without fear.

6. **Practice Information Democracy.** Without information, people cannot make responsible decisions or be held accountable for them.

7. **Reward success.** Publicly acknowledge people who demonstrate accountability.

Part Three

LET THE
REVOLUTION BEGIN

~ 11 ~

Determine Your Immediate Priorities

With the planning and foundational work behind you, the first activity in a performance management revolution is determining what your first EPM project will be. The following assessment questions may be helpful in making that decision.

Overall EPM Assessment

Question	Your Evaluation
How does your organization currently address performance management?	
What tools or applications are currently used? ☐ ERP System ☐ Point Applications ☐ Integrated EPM Suite ☐ BI Tools ☐ Spreadsheets ☐ Custom Tools	

General Assessment

Question	Your Evaluation
How well does this process work in your organization?	
Are these processes integrated? If so, how?	
Is the process integrated or dysfunctional?	
Is there a lot of rekeying of information from one system to another?	
How long is the financial closing and reporting cycle?	
When does information become available to internal management?	
Do people trust/believe in the measurement process?	
What is your vision for the organization?	
What are some of your immediate needs?	

Goal Setting

Question	Your Evaluation
How does your organization currently set and communicate corporate strategies and goals across the enterprise?	
What tools or applications are currently used? ☐ ERP System ☐ Point Applications ☐ Integrated EPM Suite ☐ BI Tools ☐ Spreadsheets ☐ Custom Tools	

General Goal Setting and Strategy

Question	Your Evaluation
How satisfied are you with your current solution?	
How long has it been in use?	
Rate the efficiency of your current goal setting/scorecarding process.	
Does your organization use any formal performance measurement or scorecarding methodology? If not, is there a defined strategic or business planning process that gets run before budgeting starts?	
How are the results of this process communicated?	
How are goals and objectives communicated down through the ranks?	
How is performance against corporate goals tracked?	
What types of metrics do you measure (financial and nonfinancial)?	
How do you hold managers accountable for achieving goals?	
How do you communicate and collaborate with each other about goals, targets, success, and concerns?	
Is compensation linked to these goals?	
Does management have the ability to "drill down" on scorecards?	
How long does management spend discussing performance each month?	
What degree of automation does your organization use?	

Question	Your Evaluation
To what extent do your scorecards/dashboards predict outcomes or future performance?	
How can the process be improved?	
What are some of your immediate needs?	

Modeling

Question	Your Evaluation
How does your organization currently handle strategic and business (or operational) modeling?	
What tools or applications are used? ☐ ERP System ☐ Point Applications ☐ Integrated EPM Suite ☐ BI Tools ☐ Spreadsheets ☐ Custom Tools	
How satisfied are you with your current solution?	
How long has it been in use?	
Rate the efficiency of your current business modeling process.	
How do you model various business scenarios and potential outcomes?	
What tools does the organization use to model organizational changes, mergers, acquisitions, divestitures, and so on?	

Question	Your Evaluation
What are some of the constraints on your business? How do you test different business scenarios against these resource constraints?	
If using spreadsheets, how do you ensure everyone is operating from a consistent set of assumptions?	
How do you measure profitability and value throughout your organization? Which products or services are most profitable?	
How do you allocate costs to various products or services?	
Are you able to use these cost drivers in your budgeting process?	
Have you adopted EVA or other value-based approaches?	
Does your organization perform any of the following cost, quality, or improvement initiatives? ☐ ABM ☐ ABC ☐ Six Sigma ☐ Baldrige Criteria ☐ Other	
Do you link operational cost models to financial performance?	
How can the process be improved?	
What are some of your immediate needs?	

Financial Planning

Question	Your Evaluation
How does your organization manage the budgeting, planning, and forecasting process?	
What type of system is your organization currently using for budgeting and planning? ☐ ERP System ☐ Point Applications ☐ Integrated EPM Suite ☐ BI Tools ☐ Spreadsheets ☐ Custom Tools	
What types of planning/budgeting does your organization perform? ☐ Strategic Planning ☐ Capital Planning ☐ Project Planning ☐ Financial Planning ☐ Headcount/Salary Planning ☐ Operational Budgeting ☐ Other	

General Planning

Question	Your Evaluation
How satisfied are you with your current solution?	
How long has it been in use?	
Rate the efficiency of your current budgeting and planning process.	

Question	Your Evaluation
Do you have a centralized or decentralized planning process?	
Can your plans and forecasts reflect changing business conditions quickly and effectively?	
What could be changed about the current process to make it more efficient?	

Budgeting Process

Question	Your Evaluation
How long does it take to complete your budgeting process?	
How often does the process happen? Are you updating budgets or forecasts on a regular basis?	
Do you have the ability to forecast and plan at the top, but at the same time empower your sites to create a detailed budget?	
Do you have to budget by projects in some cases, not just cost centers?	
How many people are involved?	
Are you involving all the right people in the process both internally and externally?	
Are you doing rolling forecasts? If so, how far out?	
How do you handle salary planning?	

Process Management

Question	Your Evaluation
Are you satisfied with the security and workflow management of your current system?	
How do you ensure the budgeting data you collect is accurate?	
How much time is spent on collecting spreadsheets, rekeying data?	
How do you manage different versions of the plans/budgets during the process?	
How do you know when everyone has turned in his or her plans/budgets?	
How many operating systems do you need to collect data from to feed into your EPM applications?	
Are data-quality management methods employed? What are they?	
Is the data-collection process integrated with the organization's compliance control procedures?	
Is the existing data-collection and transformation process fully documented with adequate controls?	

Reporting and Variance Analysis

Question	Your Evaluation
How happy are you with your ability to report on your plans/budgets?	
Can you easily look at variances for multiple years?	

Question	Your Evaluation
Do you budget at a higher or lower detail than you perform reporting?	
Do you spend more time on the mechanics of budgeting and planning or in-depth analysis?	
Are you able to create integrated financial statements in your budgeting process like cash flow statements and balance sheets? Would that be a plus?	
How can the process be improved?	
What are some of your immediate needs?	
Do your analysts, internal auditors, or external auditors ever need to reconcile between EPM and the source system from which the data originated? If so, how efficient is the process?	
Do you have confidence in the financial information generated by your existing EPM solution? If not, what do you suspect is the source for that lack of confidence?	
Do you feel you have 100 percent transparency to the source data and any processes and individuals that may have "manipulated" said data?	

Strategic Financial Planning

Question	Your Evaluation
How is cash flow modeling done, especially around debt restructuring and acquisition analysis?	
How can you reduce organization debt over the next 5 years?	

Question	Your Evaluation
How can you increase market share by 12 percent in the next 10 years?	
How can you improve how the organization is viewed by others and see that improvement reflected in the stock price or the credit rating?	
If you refinance the organization debt to more favorable terms, what impact will that have on long-term goals?	
What if you acquire another organization to increase market share?	
What if you improve the financial strength of the organization's balance sheet and cash flow?	

Monitoring

Question	Your Evaluation
How do you monitor organization performance vs. budgets, plans, and stated goals?	
What type of system is your organization currently using for performance monitoring? ☐ ERP System ☐ Point Applications ☐ Integrated EPM Suite ☐ BI Tools ☐ Spreadsheets ☐ Custom Tools	
How satisfied are you with your current solution? How long has it been in use?	

Question	Your Evaluation
How is performance against the plan measured and how often? Is there a method in place for consistent performance measurement?	
How do you find out if there are deviations from plans during execution? Are you able to make changes to plans to ensure success?	
How often do you discover challenges with execution when it is too late to make corrections?	
Where are budgets and actuals combined to enable variance reporting? How often does this happen? Quarterly? Monthly?	
Do you perform any "flash" reporting during the reporting period? How?	
Who does the analysis? How long does it take? Do you wish you had access to some information sooner?	
How is analysis on performance performed? How do you drill down from high-level variances to underlying causes?	
Do you have defined KPIs and key metrics to measure success? Financial vs. nonfinancial? Leading versus lagging indicators?	
Overall, do you feel up to date on the state of the business? How would you like to improve it?	
What are some of your immediate needs?	

Analysis

Question	Your Evaluation
What type of system is your organization currently using for analysis? ☐ ERP System ☐ Point Applications ☐ Integrated EPM Suite ☐ BI Tools ☐ Spreadsheets ☐ Custom Tools	
What kinds of analysis do you need to perform? ☐ Financial ☐ Product Profitability ☐ Call Center Analysis ☐ Supply Chain Analysis ☐ Sales Analysis ☐ HR Analysis ☐ Marketing Analysis ☐ Other	
How satisfied are you with your current solution?	
How long has your current solution been in use?	
Are these applications deployed within the same country, multiple countries same currency, multiple currencies?	
Number of users accessing these applications?	
How frequent are most of your data loads?	

Question	Your Evaluation
What analytic functionality do you need or wish you had?	
Do you understand variations and deviations in information?	
Would you like to have more insight into reported results?	
Do you wish you had more time to analyze information prior to reporting to managers or external analysts?	
Do you use the Web for users to access data?	
How can the process be improved?	
What are some of your immediate needs?	

Reporting and Financial Consolidation

Question	Your Evaluation
What type of system is your organization currently using for your reporting and consolidation application? ☐ ERP System ☐ Point Applications ☐ Integrated EPM Suite ☐ BI Tools ☐ Spreadsheets ☐ Custom Tools	

General Reporting and Financial Consolidations

Question	Your Evaluation
How satisfied are you with your current reporting/consolidation solution?	
How long has your current solution been in use?	
Rate the efficiency of your current process.	
What could be changed about the current process to make it more efficient?	
What is the length of the process to close the books and publish the numbers at your organization?	

Consolidation Process

Question	Your Evaluation
How much of that time is spent on manual processes like collecting data, rekeying data, and double-checking numbers?	
Are you able to create integrated financial statements in your reporting process like income statements, balance sheets, and cash flow statements?	
How many data sources do you need to consolidate from? What systems?	
Can you easily access information from your ERP system? Is there often a bottleneck of requests?	
Do you trust the data being submitted by remote operations?	
Do you sometimes get conflicting answers?	

Question	Your Evaluation
Do you have one version of the truth?	
How do you handle currency conversions?	
Do you have to handle complex intercompany accounting?	
Do you have any joint ventures or minority interests?	
How easy is it for you to integrate an organization post acquisition or merger?	
Considering the number of systems your organization is using to collect and manage financial information, is it difficult to get pertinent and timely answers?	
Would your organization benefit from a common place to unify the financial information and other metrics?	
How satisfied are you with your current financial consolidation solution?	

Reporting and Analysis

Question	Your Evaluation
How and when do you distribute reports within the organization?	
Once published, how and when do you distribute reports within the organization (business units, branches...)?	
Who do you report to externally, and how is this handled?	

Question	Your Evaluation
How fast can you respond to end user requests for new reports or views of information?	
How satisfied are your users with the timeliness and usefulness of the reporting and consolidation information they are receiving?	
Do you wish you had more time to analyze information?	
Do you have a common point of truth for your shared financial information? If so, how accessible is the information?	
How would you potentially cut days off your monthly closing process?	
What are some of your immediate needs?	

Data Integration

Question	Your Evaluation
Is the quality of data a concern for you?	
Do you spend time fixing errors that were caused by bad data input?	
Is the data-collection process consistent, complete, and repeatable throughout the organization?	
Do people follow a standard set of rules?	
Do you have data-mapping issues?	
Do you have complete auditability and accountability?	
Whom do you want to manage the data-collection, reconciliation, and entry process?	

Question	Your Evaluation
What method(s) do you employ to collect data?	
Does the current method provide visibility to the source data and transformation process?	
How do you audit from aggregated numbers in an analytical application down to the source GL Trial Balance? ☐ How do you answer questions? ☐ How do you investigate problems? ☐ How do you prove out balances?	
If required to comply with Sarbanes-Oxley regulation, how do you monitor your 302 and 404 processes? Are these processes integrated with your financial close process?	
Are end users who own the operating data held accountable for the data-submission and quality-validation process, leaving corporate resources to focus on value-added analysis and reporting rather than data collection and validation?	

New Pressures and Constraints

Question	Your Evaluation
Are you feeling increased pressures to publish your results faster?	
How is the shortened 10K + 10Q reporting cycle going to affect you? How will you adapt to it?	

Question	Your Evaluation
How might you cut days off your closing process?	
Do you feel comfortable signing off on your financial statements?	
Do you feel that everyone on your team is being held accountable for the completeness, accuracy, and integrity of your financial statements?	
Do you have the right level of detail to prevent or detect material misrepresentations in your financial statements?	
What impact will the Sarbanes-Oxley Act have on your organization?	
How can the process be improved?	
What are some of your immediate needs?	

Following this self-assessment, it should be clear where you believe you are excelling, where you could stand to improve, and where you need immediate assistance. Now you are ready to select your first EPM projects.

❧ 12 ❧

A Model EPM Methodology

Most of the organizations that have had success with EPM started with a pilot or a relatively small project that could be implemented quickly and deliver substantial benefits to the organization. In selecting a pilot or a small project, it helps to focus on one or more of an organization's biggest pain points. This path ensures that EPM demonstrates its value quickly and achieves visibility with a large number of people in an organization, which helps garner early support.

Many organizations concentrate initially on the finance function when deploying an EPM pilot. This gives the wider corporate culture time to observe and adjust to the philosophical shifts EPM entails.

An example of a company that took this approach to EPM is Cox Enterprises, one of the nation's leading media companies and providers of automotive services, with 2006 revenues of $13.2 billion and 80,000 employees. Aided by an organization within Cox Enterprises that supports EPM projects in its various divisions, Cox Enterprises' first foray into EPM was in its finance organization and focused on financial consolidations. With a handful of successful EPM finance-related projects completed, the group soon caught the eye of the company's radio division, Cox Radio, Inc.

Cox Radio is one of the largest radio broadcasting companies in the United States based on revenues. Cox Radio owns, operates, or provides sales and marketing services to 80 stations in 18 markets. Its radio portfolio includes 67 FM stations and 13 AM stations, and in 15 of its 18 markets, Cox Radio operates three or more stations.

In 2006, coming out of a five-year down period for the radio advertising industry, Cox Radio saw that its challenge would be driving growth in a much more competitive environment. This realization was the origin of a strategic EPM initiative to create a modern management information system that would give the company an accurate historical view of performance and a forward-looking one as well.

One of the first projects the company tackled in implementing the new system was advertising inventory. In the radio business, there is a lot of variation in the number of spots each company allows its stations to run. By that measure, Cox Radio allows fewer spots than many of its competitors, which makes managing advertising inventory a much more critical activity for Cox Radio than it might be for other companies. The ideal would be to sell as close to 100 percent of its advertising spots in any given period without actually selling out and having to turn down advertisers who wish to run ads.

To effectively manage inventory in this way would require that Cox Radio implement a system that would allow its sales team to plan, forecast, track, and report ad sales virtually on demand. In addition to implementing a robust unified platform for doing this, Cox Radio deployed interactive performance dashboards so its senior management team could add and get access to current information about advertising inventory virtually any time it wanted to.

The biggest benefit of the new inventory system is an improvement in inventory utilization and pricing. Sales managers have their compensation tied to sales, and are competitive by nature, so the new system provides incentives to maximize revenue because it provides them with the information they need to walk the delicate line between always being able to take an order and selling out.

Accuracy of planning and forecasting has also improved with the forward-looking view of demand provided by the system. In addition, senior managers are able to make better global decisions as they now have a consolidated view of demand across the company.

FOLLOW A STRUCTURED METHODOLOGY

Regardless of whether you start with a pilot, a small project, or a sequence of projects, another best practice of successful companies is to use a structured EPM methodology. A structured methodology will guide you as to how an implementation needs to be executed. It also ensures that communication is efficient and successful delivery becomes a repeatable process.

A number of different methodologies can be used, including classic "waterfall," rapid application design, agile, research and development, and so on. Regardless of which methodology you choose, a successful EPM methodology is highly structured and includes the following components (see Exhibit 12.1):

Project Management. Management of the standards across the various EPM projects and project phases.

Envision the EPM Solution. Creation and management of the overall EPM vision and strategy.

Implementation. Delivery of the EPM solution.

Education. Supporting the EPM solution in the field.

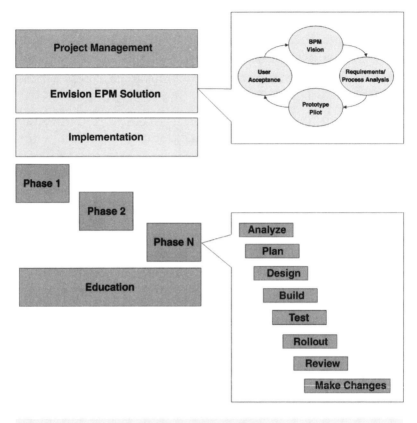

EXHIBIT 12.1 A Model EPM Methodology

ENVISION AN EPM SOLUTION

This component of the methodology delivers the most value in any EPM implementation. Envisioning the EPM solution is not a one-time effort or exercise, but rather an ongoing set of activities requiring executive support. The process becomes a cycle within itself as the EPM vision is developed and refined, and input from stakeholders is incorporated into the solution.

The first step is to define the EPM vision within your organization. The discussion begins with top management and key stakeholders creating and documenting business drivers. One method for doing this is to draw an accountability map, as discussed in a previous chapter. Mapping out the interrelationships and dependencies of key business drivers across the organization will lead to an overall EPM vision and strategy. If there are multiple groups or divisions, you will want to capture their vision as well and then map it back to an overall corporate vision, identifying gaps along the way.

Once you have the overall EPM vision, it can be broken down into business processes, subprocesses, and down even further into lower level requirements. It is during this step that a scope and charter will start to form, outlining the breakdown of the EPM vision into manageable phases and the requirements that need to addressed in each phase. This scope and charter becomes your initial roadmap.

The scope and charter will also dictate what you put into your EPM prototype. The purpose of the prototype is to provide top management with a "storyboard" on how they can measure and manage the business using the provided toolset and business processes. Having a working prototype will provide more pointed feedback if time and budget allow.

This same cycle repeats itself as feedback is collected and user acceptance is achieved. Once the implementation begins, this same cycle is used for previewing the solution out in the field. Each time a cycle is completed, the EPM vision is revised and strengthened. Top management needs to use this feedback loop to make sure the performance being measured by the solution is driving the behaviors supporting the EPM vision.

IMPLEMENTATION

When implementing EPM, it is critical to follow a highly structured process that leaves nothing to chance. We can use the classic waterfall approach to illustrate the delivery of the EPM vision consisting of an EPM solution with multiple project phases. In this example, our methodology is to include the following eight steps:

1. **Analyze.** Establish clear project success factors by defining the business and technical goals for the EPM solution, including understanding the deployment requirements, project scope, and performance capacity and planning.

2. **Plan.** Define the steps necessary to achieve a complete, implemented EPM solution.

3. **Design.** Determine detailed requirements for each component within the EPM solution, making sure all components work together to achieve the overall solution.

4. **Build.** Develop applications according to the established design.

5. **Test.** Ensure the built applications support the business processes and meet the stated performance objectives, making sure all components work together to achieve the overall EPM solution.

6. **Rollout.** Move the applications from a test or development environment to a production environment in an orderly way.

7. **Review.** Ensure the solution continues to support the stated business objectives.

8. **Make changes.** Define a process for handling changes related to the implementation.

Analyze and Plan

The analysis and planning phases of the EPM implementation are necessary to prepare for delivering all components with the EPM solution. Start by breaking out your EPM vision into smaller pieces or components, and then divide those components into manageable phases. Remember to start with small wins, but keep in mind the value of delivering the entire solution and improving performance. Balance what you can reasonably deliver to gain support toward achieving the overall vision.

The size and magnitude of the solution being delivered will dictate the amount of time you spend planning your roadmap for delivering each of the components and in which phase of the overall project. Simply put, the more time spent on these phases, the quicker and easier the deployment will be. Factors to consider include the business's strategy and vision, its technical vision, the user community, and how the EPM solution will be used.

It is critical to begin your EPM implementation with the end goals in mind. A clearly articulated strategy, with ties to the departmental goals and individual goals, is the roadmap that is required to enable a successful implementation. If each department is enabled to drive its own part of the implementation, without an overall tie to the corporate vision, the departmental agendas may be achieved, but the overall achievement of strategy will likely fail. Tying day-to-day operations to the organization's strategy is critical to the success of the EPM initiative.

Stakeholders and executive sponsors working with the EPM initiative leaders can help to ensure the vision and strategy have been clearly articulated and visualized. This will enable the leaders to prioritize the phases of implementation to ensure the largest payback and adoption rate, and ensure the most pressing business issues are addressed first.

Know your systems—apply technology with wisdom.

Implementing EPM is more than just buying technology. If the implementation is viewed as strictly a technology exercise, it will likely fail. If the initiative leaders and/or their IT partners have not done their homework, they might try to take this path and simply call on their favorite vendors to sell them the systems they don't currently have.

The importance of technology is not to be under-stated, however. A paper-based or nonintegrated EPM is also likely to fail. A better approach would be to assess your existing systems and match them to your EPM require-ments. Where you lack the necessary technology to enable a performance-accountable organization, consider purchas-ing new technology.

There are numerous technology companies out there with many solutions to fit countless situations. Remember to research them thoroughly and ensure that they and their solutions are sound, and proven.

EPM Solution Selection

Integration versus ease of use and functionality is the classic balancing act the business users and IT grapple with daily. For EPM to be successful, both sides must be taken into account and implemented equally.

Best-of-breed software typically has the best depth of functionality and nice user interfaces, but software suites tend to have tighter integration. So, what is the right choice? There are EPM focused vendors that can provide both—and provide them in balance. These vendors also tend to empower the business users by enabling them to do more complex tasks through an end-user interface, thus reducing dependency on IT for mundane and time-consuming tasks, and freeing up IT for more strategically focused initiatives.

To illustrate the nature of the choice, consider the case of a large European telecommunications company. The company had previously used individual applications from various suppliers in its subsidiary companies to support financial management tasks including budgeting, analysis, and reporting. Then, the company chose to implement EPM software as part of a cost-savings initiative that included a reduction in the number of its technology vendors, optimization of IT architecture, and an improved rate of return on technology investments.

After assessing its options, the company determined that it needed a comprehensive solution to meet its holistic needs for budgeting, planning, analysis, and reporting, and score-carding and monitoring. This naturally led it to implement an integrated suite of EPM applications across the enterprise instead of disconnected applications in individual groups and departments.

Regardless of how you make the decision, it's critical to select the right EPM tool. An organization needs to make sure it considers both organizational/strategic and technical requirements and follows a selection process to make sure it makes good vendor choices based on a broad view of the organization and its needs. The tool(s) selected need to offer the breadth, depth, and scalability necessary for the organization's users to carry on its business. For most or-ganizations, the next-generation planning technology must possess the following attributes:

- Dynamic/real-time updates
- Multitiered aggregation and granularity
- Integration with enterprise applications and data sources
- Translation between financial and nonfinancial metrics
- Enhanced creation and management of "what-if" models
- Real-time display and communication of informa-tion.

The rapid adoption of EPM is fueled by a drive to empower the masses with powerful planning, reporting, and analysis tools—achieving Information Democracy. The EPM solution should leverage the Web to provide a scalable, secure, and reliable EPM infrastructure.

Design

In the design phase, you should create design documents that summarize your organization's business and technical vision and your deployment strategy. Remember to tie these design documents back to the overall delivery of the EPM solution. Ask how each design affects or leverages the others. Make sure you're consistent with the other components on your delivery roadmap. While you design each individual component and start to generate test cases, keep in mind that the component needs to be tested as part of the overall EPM solution as well.

Another element to keep in mind is that the people responsible for building the application are usually different from those responsible for designing the system. Therefore, it is important that the documentation (including detailed dimension architecture, detailed calculation design, project path with time line, and resources) be as comprehensive as possible.

The main components of the design phase include:

- An EPM component checkpoint
- Designing the plan and environment for testing
- Designing security
- Designing the migration plan
- Designing the training plan
- Establishing rollout criteria

Build

After a complete design is discussed and documented, the next step is implementing the design. This phase includes:

- **EPM component checkpoint**—Design the deployment while considering all solutions being implemented.

- **Implementing the application**—Implement the design of the application detailed in the design phase.

- **Developing a proof of concept (where it makes sense)**—Create a proof of concept to validate certain functionality and distribute to a subset of the user community for testing and feedback. The conceptual proof can also be used for preliminary performance and scalability testing.

- **Implementing security**—Implement the user setup and security assignments that were detailed in the design phase.

- **Developing support processes**—Develop support processes to document the use of the application for end users and administrative processes that help update and maintain the solution. The main components of the support processes include application, end user, administrator, maintenance of hardware, and maintenance of software.

- **Creating testing scripts**—Create the testing scripts for the various types of testing scenarios that will be performed for functional, system, and performance testing.

- **Developing a training program**—Identify resources for training, specifics for training, and coordinate the training process.

Test

After building the application, you can start validating the solution to ensure it meets the needs of the business, and the architecture of the environment can support the solution. You can use different types of tests to validate the solution. This phase must be completed so the rollout phase can be initiated with full knowledge of the performance-testing results. The solution should also be tested against the EPM vision to ensure the component works as defined in the Analyze and Plan phase.

The main components of the testing phase should include:

- **EPM Communication Checkpoint**—Designing the deployment while considering all solutions being implemented.
- **Functional Testing**—Ensuring correct results are provided when executing calculations, data entry, report retrieval, consolidation, and so on.
- **System Testing**—Perform an end-to-end process test to ensure all the individual components are compatible with each other.
- **User Acceptance Testing (UAT)**—Ensure the solution has met the needs of the end users from a functional and performance perspective.
- **Performance Testing**—Determine if the solution meets the performance goals that were highlighted in the design phase, and ensure the appropriate hardware architecture has been implemented to support the solution.

Rollout

After the system has been tested to validate sizing and performance, it can be rolled out into production. To maintain optimal performance, the following must be monitored:

- **EPM Communication Checkpoint**—Designing the deployment while considering all solutions being implemented.
- **Training of end users**—Run the training scripts identified in the design and build phases.

- **Completing and communicating support processes**—Implement the support processes designed in the Build phase, and communicate these processes to end users and administrators.
- Go live.

Here is a Production Environment checklist that may be helpful to you.

Production Environment Checklist

Task	Status
Ensure UAT is completed.	
Review partial testing results, if available.	
Review application rollout plan and accomplishments.	
Review outstanding issues.	
Verify the contingency plan (readiness).	
Verify available backup system and processes.	
Process final historical data conversions and updates to production environment.	
Synchronize test environment to production.	
Assess production environment readiness.	
Send go-live recommendation to executive sponsor.	
Deploy business process and procedures.	
Deploy internal support policy and procedures.	
Communicate availability of solutions to users.	

Review

After the application has been deployed, review it to ensure there is an evaluation of how the plan for the solution was executed. This review phase should include:

- **EPM Communication Checkpoint**—Design the deployment while considering all solutions being implemented.
- **Project review**—Review the completed solution against the initial goals and requirements.
- **Future implementation phase**—Discuss what the future phases will encompass, including goals and objectives, and what the proposed solution will be.

Make Changes

You will also need a process in place to handle changes related to the EPM solution. Changes can take different forms and have various impacts on the solution. When the change is identified, it is imperative that the change management process be followed to ensure all the necessary phases are reviewed before a change is brought into production. This process is iterative and should be executed in its entirety to ensure all potential impacts are addressed.

The main types of changes that might be made to the EPM solution can be categorized into three groups:

- Business process or user activity or configuration change
- Technical (hardware and software)
- Users

It is important to document the details of the final and evolving system. Whether you have a new implementation or are re-executing change management, this practice is necessary for sustaining a successful deployment.

EDUCATION

Effective education is one of the best ways to ensure the successful implementation and utilization of your solution—and to get greater business value and results from the technology faster. Education provides comprehensive training solutions that give the client workforce the knowledge and skills they need to optimize performance of their EPM solution and help speed ROI. You should look for a mixture of the blended curriculum combining intensive, hands-on instructor-led training with self-paced computer-based training. If budget allows, you can go one step further with a custom learning solution to help ensure all members—administrators, developers, managers, power users, end users, and IT personnel—receive the right training at the right time.

CHANGE MANAGEMENT

Implementing EPM means change. An organization may change the content or format of information provided to employees, its business processes, and/or the expected behavior of employees, and possibly change the metrics for evaluating employees' performance. To successfully manage these changes, an organization needs to properly plan for coping with them. By following the best practices listed in the next section, companies can increase the likelihood of success of their EPM implementation.

Ensure a Supportive Organizational Environment

No matter how technically proficient an organization is, an EPM implementation will not be successful without a supportive organizational environment. To achieve this, it is necessary to:

- Build a broad-based consensus in advance of the implementation for a change in both technology and culture
- Align strategic goals with operational objectives
- Shift business paradigms based on EPM
- Align EPM with business strategy
- Have the business areas *partner* with IT departments in ownership, and help guide the IT project teams
- Communicate with and engage all relevant business areas

Ensure Sufficient Funding and Resources

Implementing EPM requires an appropriate financial budget and human resources attributed to the project. Often, backing is underestimated because, in the eyes of some businesspeople, EPM is mistakenly seen as simply a different way of reporting. As such, they expect the cost to be more in line with a new reporting tool rather than an enterprisewide system.

To ensure success, funds must be secured with an enterprise-based deployment in mind—which will include enterprisewide software for enablement.

If the EPM project is already underway and you are facing the situation of inadequate funds to complete the project successfully, there are viable options. Success is often measured in terms of user adoption, so you could consider focusing on specific functionality that will help a larger number of users (say budgeting and planning functions) to solve a broad business pain (more accurate and timely budgets). Once the pain is resolved, and adoption is successful, you can use that success to garner additional funds to add more functionality to solve another business pain.

This type of phased approach breeds a loyal following that makes moving to the next phase easier. This phased approach is sometimes referred to as the "start anywhere" approach.

Obtain Employee Buy-In

Deployment of EPM is not successful until EPM is widely used. As part of its EPM implementation plan, an organization needs to consider and make specific plans to ensure user acceptance.

Getting users to accept and use EPM often requires commitment and a culture change at the very highest levels of the organization. Therefore, executive sponsorship and support is critical to success in defining and owning the overall EPM vision and strategy.

Other actions that will help ensure user adoption include:

- Pegging compensation to successful use of EPM
- Aggressive marketing of the new EPM solution within the organization, including promoting successes
- Defining and promoting links between tactical execution and strategic management
- Providing appropriate user training and reinforcing it on an ongoing basis
- Designing the implementation with ease of use for business users as a top priority, including the use of dashboards and scorecards

You should expect resistance to a new EPM tool or performance methodology, with the greatest resistance coming from individuals who have the most invested in the old tool or methodology. Those most likely to feel that investment—and most likely to resist something new—are probably the people with the most valuable IT skills and organizational knowledge. Getting them on board first will make it easier to convince others of the value of the changes.

Advice from the Trenches

The majority of the organizations that have implemented EPM projects believe that success is as much about change management as it is about processes and systems.

For example, the project manager at a technology consulting firm that built a EPM portal reported that it actually took more time to get management on board than to implement the project. And after that, its partners and principals had to become more comfortable accessing reports online versus a paper book.

User involvement ranks high as a critical success factor. One Center of Excellence leader in a manufacturing company recommends strong partnership with internal users, noting that it's important to learn their language, sit with them, and learn their business to earn their respect and support.

A project manager at a major airline suggests keeping project requirements realistic and attainable and to keep the 80/20 rule in mind, which is that 80 percent of the functionality can be produced for 20 percent of the cost. This would suggest keeping it simple to get fast, robust systems that are relatively inexpensive to implement and maintain.

The project manager at the large transportation company, whose dashboard implementation I mentioned earlier, recommends that requirements be written into a formal document. A formal charter, scope, and project requirements tell your internal users what you're going to build for them. In addition, many of your internal customers are going to try to tell you what they want you to do, so it's important to write and communicate a detailed project plan.

The project manager also recommends planning for the future from the very beginning, noting that if you build your first application correctly, test it thoroughly, and store it as a module, you can reuse it for future projects.

The project manager at the electronics retailer referenced in this book as a company that leveraged its compliance initiative into a performance management initiative, put user training at the top of the list of success factors, noting that if users don't like an application, they won't use it.

Finally, nearly all project leaders stress the need for communication. The project manager of the pharmaceutical company whose scorecarding application was mentioned in this book, suggests that overcommunicating is just not possible.

Prepare for Some (Pleasant) Surprises

For all the challenges and the need to plan and implement carefully, some unexpected benefits usually come out of EPM projects. Consider the case of Pearson, an international media company, owner of highly regarded assets such as the *Financial Times* and Penguin, and Pearson Education, the world's largest education company, with operations all over the world, more than 29,000 employees, and dual listings in the United Kingdom and the United States.

A highly decentralized and growing company with business units that prize their independence, Pearson's assignment was to set consistent criteria for managing financial performance in line with world-class standards.

In particular, Pearson found that making changes in its existing financial-management system was disruptive, so the company had wait until its year-end close to make them. This meant devising elaborate workarounds during the course of the year to deal with new disclosure requirements or management information changes. Each change and its workaround would cascade throughout the global organization based on local reporting requirements and systems outside of those at corporate. In this complex organization, headquarters required new tools for sustained access and visibility.

In implementing a new EPM financial-management system, Pearson's goals were to accelerate reporting, streamline processes, and provide a single, centralized source of management information that could cope with a broad range of financial and operational KPIs. The new system delivered on these goals and on some unexpected benefits as well.

For example, individual reporting entities—each with its own charts of accounts and local finance systems—automatically populate into a uniform companywide reporting chart of accounts. The local businesses can use the new system for their own reporting needs while the company uses it for companywide financial consolidations. The smoothing of the data collection and reporting processes means that Pearson has been able to reduce its monthly reporting cycle from 20 days to six days.

Also, maintaining the system has proven easier than first anticipated. With the new process, it is possible to make controlled, approved changes anytime to security, metadata or rules, and all business units have the updates at the same time. A great example of this is the update in accounting policies for GAAP reporting under IFRS as well as Sarbanes-Oxley compliance.

~ 13 ~

Measuring Outcomes

It is well known that metrics can tell you anything you want. For every event, metrics can be developed that present different—even opposing—conclusions. Getting metrics right is one of the hardest things to achieve with EPM. And underestimating the impact of metrics is the biggest reason why EPM initiatives fail or underdeliver.

Most people tasked with EPM understand how important it is to design the right management processes. They know you can't do this without adequate technology and a proper framework—be that the Balanced Scorecard, Value-Based Management, or Six Sigma. But often, organizations just don't pay enough attention to getting the metrics right.

As the adage goes, "What gets measured gets done." The right metrics drive the right behavior, and the wrong metrics drive the wrong behavior. In fact, just putting measurements in place at all affects behavior. This phenomenon is known as the Hawthorne Effect[1]

The Hawthorne Effect was developed based on experiences conducted at the Hawthorne Plant of the Western Electric Company near Chicago between 1927 and 1932 to measure productivity in relation to changes in working

---

[1]The study of workers at the Hawthorne Plant was conducted by Harvard Business School Professor Elton Mayo and his associates, F. J. Roethlisberger and William J. Dickson.

conditions. Researchers found that when the lights in the factory were brightened, productivity increased. When the lights were dimmed, productivity also increased. And when the lights were returned to normal levels, productivity increased yet again. Bottom line, researchers concluded that the fact that workers knew measurements were taking place made them work harder.

Not understanding the impact of metrics on behavior often leads people to "game the numbers." Here are a few examples:

Unbalanced metrics. "Let's do whatever we can to get customers to pay up immediately, so we improve our Days Sales Outstanding—even if it ruffles a few feathers."

Rewarding wrong behavior. "Let's spend surplus budget on a new project in December or the budget will be lost."

Artificial deadlines. "The deadline for making my target is the end of the year. I still have five months to wait for a miracle."

Conflicting objectives. "Fifty percent of my time is allocated to this project, but if I spend 80 percent of my time working for my line manager, I will still get a good review."

Window dressing. "People are our most important asset. Let's eliminate 10 percent of them after the second bad quarter."

The problem with these behaviors is not bad people; the problem is bad metrics. Often, the process is just too clinical. A management team reviews the business objectives that need to be met. It comes up with a list of metrics that describe the objectives and chooses a few, based on available data or what they think they can most easily measure.

Designing the right metrics should be influenced by what behaviors you are trying to stimulate and which ones we are trying to avoid. Here are some examples of the right way to set and enforce metrics.

PROVIDE FEEDBACK

We all know from personal life that feedback drives behavior. It is important to hear how we are doing and how we are perceived. Organizations are no different.

Let's take an example. A claims department of an insurance company each day sorted claims by U.S. postal ZIP code and distributed them to Group North, East, West, and South. The most important performance indicator was "average processing time per claim," and this metric needed improvement. Senior management decided to publish a weekly graph of claims processing production by group on the message board near the coffee machine. No change management program and no management by objectives; just feedback through the graph.

After just a few weeks, the effects were visible. Group West's average time was sagging because two staff members in Group West were ill, so Group East offered to help by taking over a load of claims. At the same time, Group East counted on the help of the others for the next two weeks while a few employees were on vacation. The workload began to balance itself automatically and the average processing time decreased. Feedback clearly drove behavior.

ALIGN PERSONAL AND
CORPORATE OBJECTIVES

Most salespeople are measured on revenue and indicators like customer retention and customer satisfaction. Although revenue is an important corporate objective, profitability often matters most. Many CFOs complain that margins are under pressure because salespeople offer too many discounts. But this is caused by personal objectives that are misaligned with corporate objectives.

A much better sales target would be profitability or, if profitability analysis on a per transaction basis is too complicated, contribution margin. Contribution margin consists of revenue minus direct costs, such as the cost of goods sold or the cost of sales. With this model, when a customer asks for a discount, the salesperson has a mindset that is in tune with the overall objectives, and can therefore contribute more directly to overall profitably.

COMBINE EPM AND ENTERPRISE RISK MANAGEMENT

In most organizations, EPM and risk management are seen as separate disciplines. But EPM and enterprise risk management (ERM) are related. EPM has KPIs; ERM has key risk indicators. The Balanced Scorecard—the most well-known EPM methodology—speaks to the financial, customer, and process growth of a company; ERM distinguishes financial, customer, and operational risk.

There are multiple advantages to combining EPM and ERM. First, ERM allows the organization to establish improvement projects before EPM metrics show that a problem is looming. Second, ERM challenges the intuitive belief of EPM that everything will proceed as planned. Lastly, risk management prepares an organization much better for dealing with discontinuities that threaten corporate objectives.

ANTICIPATE BEHAVIORS

Every organization has its own behaviors—some constructive and some not. It is important to understand nonconstructive behaviors, as they may keep a company from acting correctly upon strategic objectives and measurements.

One privatized public service organization decided to introduce KPIs. The initiative was widely resisted, as various districts felt this was violating the privacy of districts and their employees. The CFO pushed forward and noticed that, contrary to all theory, performance of the highest scoring districts went down, instead of overall performance going up. Upon investigation, it was discovered that the worse scoring districts were accusing the best scoring districts of making them look bad. This led to a change for the worse in the behavior of the better scoring districts to create an equal, albeit lower, performance.

REWARD THE RIGHT BEHAVIORS

People who show they are doing the right thing should be publicly rewarded. Every month, a professional services firm held a sales meeting. In one meeting, a sales manager spoke up and said that he would most likely not make his sale target if his number of orders didn't increase. The other salespeople thought he had ruined his chance of receiving a bonus because he still had more than six months to make the target.

But senior management praised the sales manager for having the courage to step forward and ask for help. Immediately, two presales consultants were assigned to the sales manager, the COO promised to tour his region, and the sales manager was awarded a special incentive for loyalty. The other salespeople stood corrected and learned a valuable lesson.

DEFINE METRICS THAT DRIVE THE RIGHT BEHAVIORS

The theory is clear: Metrics and targets should be assigned to a performance owner, and that person should have the means to achieve those targets. But conventional wisdom isn't always right. Some key metrics should not be assigned to a single performance owner, but to two or sometimes three performance owners who need to collaborate to achieve the target. In this case, the targets are not defined for a single business domain, but for crossovers between multiple areas—the business interfaces.

For example, a CIO had a problem with the business interface between IT Development and IT Operations. IT Development was responsible for implementing systems, and IT Operations was responsible for running them, after extensive acceptance testing. A new metric was introduced: average time used to take a new function point into production. Both managers complained that they did not have the means to achieve the target by themselves. The CIO pointed out that they had hit the nail on the head. The metric served to drive collaborative behavior.

Bottom line, if you simply follow conventional wisdom, metrics can tell you after the fact whether you have achieved results. Done right, metrics can actually drive the behaviors that lead to sound business results. And that is when EPM reaches maturity as a performance-management tool.

Afterword

Altimeters. Vertical speed indicators. Fuel gauges. Airplanes have an endless array of instrumentation to tell pilots what is going on while they're flying through the sky. But pilots get into trouble when they rely too heavily on these tools and forget to look out the window.

By the same token, EPM is an awesome set of instruments for knowing how a business is performing and for taking action in the future. But EPM today is based on KPIs for business that are relevant today. And there may be something coming at you head-on that you just can't see with existing performance metrics.

While tracking and projecting performance based on existing metrics is essential, it's not enough if companies want to remain competitive and relevant in the future. Professionals need to continually ask themselves original questions—questions outside of their day-to-day reality—that can lead to fresh thinking, new business opportunities, and readiness for unplanned events.

I call this "decision context." Decision context is the information we use to color our judgment of significant issues. The key is to identify and play out a number of possible scenarios—including highly unusual ones—before they happen in an effort to uncover new insights and be prepared for the unexpected.

DIFFERENT THINKING

Although there are many techniques for thinking differently about the business, I like the approach used by the futurist and business strategist Peter Schwarz in his book, *The Art of the Long View.* Using Schwarz's methodology, you start with an important question, and then identify and group determining factors into various categories—political, economic, social, technological, physical, and so on. It's critical when you develop these factors that you think beyond the constraints of today. It's also important to force yourself to think outside of the box when imaging future scenarios.

Next, you select two significant factors that are independent of each other—in other words, neither one can be the cause or result of the other. It's always tempting to evaluate multiple factors, but as humans, two is often all we can really handle. Plus, it's actually harder than you might think to isolate three or more factors that are completely independent of one another.

Armed with these two significant yet independent factors, the next step is to brainstorm how these factors might be made to relate to one another in the context of a future business opportunity or threat.

CONNECTING NEW DOTS

I recently participated in a roundtable discussion with several distinguished business executives and academics where we put this technique to work in a hypothetical situation.

It happened that within three of the companies represented, real estate was a major opportunity for them, so we decided this would be an interesting area to explore.

Using Schwarz's technique of selecting two significant factors that are independent of each other, we chose to brainstorm mobility (the desire and the ability to travel) and telecommuting (the option of working away from an office setting).

Not only did we enjoy a stimulating and creative discussion, in the course of our brainstorming session, we also discovered a new business opportunity we all found quite intriguing.

The new business we envisioned was a vacation-telecommuting destination resort. Travelers—most likely high-income, single professionals—would spend several months at an exotic location where they would receive all the personal services they have come to expect. These destinations would provide a workspace, an Internet connection, technical support, video conferencing, large screen monitors—you name it. They would also arrange for social opportunities, outings, and receptions. (These travelers are, after all, single.) And of course, they'd be located in some of the most desirable spots in the world.

We ended our brainstorm there, but it's not difficult to guess what the next steps might be for an organization seriously interested and in a position to pursue our idea as a new business opportunity.

Interesting stuff, but how does it relate to EPM?

In a perfect world, EPM starts at the inception of a business idea and helps it get better over time. This is easier when you have observations of the real world: You can measure them. Much of it has to do with documenting assumptions. We state what we believe and then start collecting data to test and validate that belief. Then we adjust the model as we learn more.

But truly great business ideas are rarely sparked by analyzing the current reality. So, what is the role of EPM when we can't observe anything helpful in the real world because nothing exists yet? The answer is, EPM can kick start the process. If company profits are off, sales are down, or quality is decreasing, performance data may be the wake-up call to explore things more fully. Companies also need to think creatively about positive performance metrics—not just those that are alarming.

EPM also plays a critical role once new business ideas have been conceived. Before investing heavily in an initiative, companies must model the concept. They need a plan, including revenue goals, people requirements, business processes, and equipment and so on. These must all be tracked with EPM.

With new initiatives, it is especially critical that everyone is in tight alignment. This is precisely where Information Democracy fits in. Information Democracy, as a principle of equality that demands actionable insight for all, requires that information is shared among all who may benefit from it— line of business managers, marketing managers, HR managers, and so on—and not be hoarded by the IT department or the executive suite. With EPM, all the players in a new business initiative know what they are responsible for and how they are meeting those responsibilities.

RESIST THE STATUS QUO

New ideas can be wholly threatening to the status quo within a company. In organizations, just as in our personal lives, we tend to surround ourselves with people like us. This can lead to a form of organizational blindness that prevents new ideas from flourishing.

When the pilgrims neared the shores of the Atlantic, the Native Americans simply could not see them. They had no context for humans appearing from the ocean, so they were blind to their existence. Companies are the same. They optimize and become so good at the current reality that they often can't see beyond it.

This is why it's so essential to stay open to new ideas— and proactively develop them. Step outside of yourself as much as possible to understand and leverage the world around you. Make new connections by reading science fiction novels, medical journals, or biographies of Napoleon. Anything that's indirectly related to your daily focus.

Remember, you can analyze all you want—and I encourage you to do so—but there is a diminishing return on the current reality. Place some bets. Have a willingness to be wrong. Take a chance.

And above all, unlike the pilot who relies too much on instrumentation, don't forget to look out the window.

Appendix: EPM Resources

Organizations
BPM Standards Group
BPM Forum
The Data Warehousing Institute

Vendor and Consultant Listings
Business Finance magazine: Vendor Directory—
www.businessfinancemag.com/resources/
vendors/index.html

Business Finance magazine: 2007 Business Performance
Management Software Buyers Guide—
www.businessfinancemag.com/magazine/
archives/article.html?articleID=
14745&highlight=technology%20buyers%20guides

The *OLAP Report*—www.olapreport.com

BPM Magazine—www.bpmmag.net

Useful Links
Business Intelligence Network—
www.b-eye-network.com/home/

Ohio State University, Fisher College of Business, Center
for Business Performance Management—
http://fisher.osu.edu/centers/cbpm/

Publications

BPM magazine

Business Finance Magazine

DM Review

Intelligent Enterprise

Glossary

Balanced Scorecard A performance-achievement framework developed by Robert S. Kaplan and David P. Norton that required performance-measurement systems to identify measures and objectives related to four perspectives: financial, customer, internal process and learning, and growth.

Basel II An effort by international banking supervisors to update the original international bank capital accord (Basel I), which has been in effect since 1988. The revised accord aims to improve the consistency of capital regulations internationally, make regulatory capital more risk sensitive, and promote enhanced risk-management practices among large, internationally active banking organizations.

Business Intelligence (BI) Knowledge gained through the access and analysis of business information.

Business Intelligence Tools The tools and technologies used to access and analyze business information. They include tools for query and reporting, OLAP (online analytical processing), data mining and advanced analytics, end-user tools for ad hoc query and analysis, enterprise-class query, analysis, and reporting, including dashboards, for performance-monitoring and production reporting against all enterprise data sources.

Enterprise Performance Management A category of technologies and practices that enables organizations to translate strategies into plans, monitor execution, and provide insight to improve financial and operational performance. The research and analyst firm Gartner describes this category as "Corporate Performance Management," which it uses as an umbrella term to describe the methodologies, metrics processes, and systems used to monitor and manage the business performance of an enterprise. AMR Research calls the category "Enterprise Performance Management," which it describes as an emerging superset of applications and processes that cross traditional department boundaries to manage the full life cycle of business decision making.

Business Modeling The process of creating models of how a business works and functions in such a way that they can be used productively to simulate the real world. The ability of executives, planners, managers, and analysts to model and test operational and financial planning assumptions for their business is fundamental to good decision making.

EPM Center of Excellence An EPM Center of Excellence solves many of the challenges faced by organizations implementing EPM. It is an internal group that provides consulting services and oversees the EPM efforts within an organization. The CoE helps standardize tools, procedures, and best practices, enabling companies to leverage their experiences across projects, allowing them to achieve scalable results and reduce the cost of their EPM efforts.

Consolidation The process of taking data from different systems and entities and possibly disparate formats, and combine and aggregate that information to create a unified view.

Dashboard An application or custom user interface that organizes and presents information in a graphical format that is easy to read. The information may be integrated from multiple components into a unified display. A dashboard metaphor is useful for conveying the idea. The difference is that in EPM, the dashboard is interactive. A dashboard helps monitor individual, business unit, and organizational performance and processes for a greater understanding of the business.

Data Mart A system for collecting data from transactional systems and aggregating it in a data store for access by decision makers. Typically involves some scrubbing or cleansing of data as it is extracted and loaded from transactional systems to ensure consistency of the data (e.g., normalizing customer names). Data marts are departmental in scope and are used to isolate the data needed to support a particular division or department's needs. This data may come directly from transactional systems or represent a subset of the data warehouse.

Data Manipulation Language (DML) The underlying language for accessing and controlling a database management system. Examples include SQL (Structured Query Language) for relational and MDX (Multi-Dimensional Expression Language) for multidimensional database-management systems.

Data Warehouse A data-collection and organization system, similar to a data mart, but designed to work on an enterprise level.

Decision Support System (DSS) Business analytics presented in a format appropriate for use by executives in making decisions.

Economic Capital (EC) The amount of capital that banks and insurance companies set aside as a buffer against potential losses from their business activities.

Economic Capital Modeling The process by which models are created of the optimal use of economic capital across a company, including the appropriate capital to support specific business units and activities and to quantify how changes in strategy alter capital requirements.

Economic Value Added (EVA) A "value-based" metric popular with many companies, EVA is an integrated framework for performance measurement, value-based planning, and incentive compensation developed by Joel Stern and G. Bennett Stewart III. EVA is calculated by taking operating profits and deducting a charge for the cost of capital. The Stern Stewart EVA framework is now employed by more than 300 companies worldwide, including Coca-Cola, Siemens, Sony, and government agencies such as the U.S. Postal Service and The Port of Singapore Authority. Companies that have adopted EVA frequently realize long-lasting improvements in operating efficiency, growth, morale, motivation, and stock market value.

Enterprise Resource Planning (ERP) A transactional software system that allows a company to automate and integrate the majority of its business processes, to share common data and practices across the enterprise.

Enterprise Risk Management (ERM) Enables organizations to assess and analyze risk holistically, identifying areas of concern, and proactively developing measures to comply with regulations.

Event-Driven Planning A planning process that is focused on significant events as opposed to arbitrary calendar dates.

GAAP Stands for Generally Accepted Accounting Practices and is the standard framework of guidelines for financial accounting. It includes the standards, conventions, and rules accountants follow in recording and summarizing transactions, and in the preparation of financial statements.

IFRS Stands for International Financial Reporting Standards and is a set of new accounting and financial reporting standards developed by an international committee in the early 2000s that supersede IAS (International Account Standards) that were adopted beginning in the 1970s.

Information Democracy The concept of delivering actionable insight to all user constituents. Similar to information transparency, except that Information Democracy suggests an action step once an insight has been gleaned.

Key Performance Indicator (KPI) A measurement, or metric, that is included on a scorecard because it drives performance achievement. Key performance indicators express objectives in financial units for comparative purposes. Financial information can be used to compare results and thus measure performance.

Lean A business system for organizing and managing product development, operations, suppliers, and customer relations that stresses creating customer value with less human effort, less space, less capital, and less time than the traditional system of mass production.

Master Data Data that is shared across systems (such as lists or hierarchies of customers, suppliers, accounts, or organizational units) and is used to classify and define transactional data. Many companies currently manage their master data in a very manual fashion (via spreadsheets), in a homegrown system, or in some cases do not manage it at all.

OLAP (Online Analytical Processing) The process of manipulating large chunks of data in response to analytical queries by end users. OLAP data is organized by dimensions (time, products, geographies, measures, scenarios, and so on) that include hierarchies, which support drilling down from higher levels to more detailed views. OLAP gives analysts, managers, and executives insight into data through fast, consistent, interactive access to a wide variety of possible views of information. OLAP technology enables data to be explored well beyond the capabilities of traditional reporting systems.

Performance-Accountable Organization An organization that delivers continuous performance improvement and accountability in all its activities, from all its employees, across the enterprise. When an organization is truly performance accountable, CEOs and CFOs can report openly and comprehensively on performance and set expectations with confidence.

Performance Scorecard A strategic management tool designed to translate an organization's mission statement and overall business strategy into specific, quantifiable goals and to monitor the organization's overall performance—not just financial returns—so that future performance can be predicted and proper actions taken to create the desired future.

Predictive Modeling The process by which models are created or chosen to try to best predict an outcome.

Risk Adjusted Return on Capital (RAROC) Modeling The process by which models are created to evaluate projects and investments that are deemed riskier than their low-risk or riskless counterparts.

Rolling Forecast A forecasting method that shifts planning away from historic budgeting and forecasting, and moves it toward a continuous predictive modeling method. It requires access to relevant information from multiple data sources and business processes throughout the enterprise.

Sarbanes-Oxley On July 30, 2002, the Sarbanes-Oxley Act (Public Law 104–204) went into effect and changed the corporate landscape in the United States with regard to financial reporting and auditing for publicly traded companies. Written to address many of the issues brought to light during the incidents involving Enron and Arthur Andersen, the law establishes stringent financial reporting requirements for companies doing business in the United States.

Scorecard An application or custom user interface that helps manage an organization's performance by optimizing and aligning organizational units, business processes, and individuals. It should also provide internal and industry benchmarks, and goals and targets that help individuals understand their contributions to the organization. The use of scorecards spans the operational, tactical, and strategic aspects of the business and its decisions. Often, methodologies derived from internal best practices, or an external industry methodology, are used for scorecarding. (For example, the term "The Balanced Scorecard" specifically refers to the Kaplan and Norton methodology.)

Six Sigma A rigorous and disciplined methodology that uses data and statistical analysis to measure and improve a company's operational performance by identifying and eliminating "defects" in manufacturing and service-related processes.

Service Oriented Architecture (SOA) A collection of services that communicate with each other. The services are self-contained and do not depend on the context or state of the other service.

Value-based Management (VBM) Reporting An approach to management and performance reporting that aligns a company's overall aspirations, analytical techniques, and management processes to focus decision making on the drivers of value.

Virtual Close The ability to complete the entire closing and reporting cycle within a few hours instead of days or even weeks.

Voice of the Customer (VOC) A Six Sigma process for capturing the requirements and feedback from customers (internal or external) to provide them with the best in class service/product quality. This process stresses being proactive and constantly innovative to capture the changing requirements of the customers over time.

Index